Dogwood and Catnip

Dogwood and Catnip

LIVING TRIBUTES TO PETS WE HAVE LOVED AND LOST

Marsha Olson

Fairview Press
Minneapolis

Published by Fairview Press, 2450 Riverside Avenue, Minneapolis, MN 55454. Fairview Press is a division of Fairview Health Services, a community-focused health system providing a complete range of services, from the prevention of illness and injury to care for the most complex medical conditions. For a free catalog of Fairview Press books, call toll-free 800-544-8207, or visit our Web site at www.fairviewpress.org.

Library of Congress Cataloging-in-Publication Data

Olson, Marsha, 1955–

Dogwood and catnip : living tributes to pets we have loved and lost / Marsha Olson.

p.   cm.

ISBN 1–57749–133–5 (pbk. : alk. paper)

1. Sanctuary gardens. 2. Gardens—Symbolic aspects. 3. Gardens—Religious aspects. 4. Pet owners—Psychology. 5. Pets—Death—Psychological aspects. 6. Bereavement—Psychological aspects. I. Title

SB454.3.S25 O478 2003

712—dc21   2003002488

First printing: May 2003

Printed in the United States of America

07 06 05 04 03   7 6 5 4 3 2 1

Cover: Laurie Ingram Design

Photo credits: frontispiece, p. 114 courtesy of Lane Stiles; pp. 2, 3 courtesy of June Lynne Mucci; pp. 6, 7 (and back cover) courtesy of Marge Loyd; pp. 10, 13 courtesy of Sybil Allison Graham; pp. 14, 20, 21, 85, 87, 89 (and back cover) courtesy of Brenda Olson Dunbar; pp. 16, 17 courtesy of Abigail Marie Coyour; pp. 22, 23 courtesy of Andrew Dominic Psyhos; pp. 24, 75, 80, 101, 118 courtesy of Royce Dunbar; pp. 26, 27 courtesy of Kathy Kromm; pp. 30, 31 courtesy of Elyn Zerfas; pp. 70, 71 courtesy of Aleta Hogan; pp. 90, 91 (and back cover) courtesy of Diane Newman; lower-left photo on p. 95 courtesy of Marilyn Nelson; p. 100 courtesy of Michelle Raye and Texstone of British Columbia, Canada; pp. 104, 105 courtesy of Sandra Laemmle; pp. 110, 111 courtesy of Sandra S. Nelson; pp. 115, 117 courtesy of Judith A. Ruta; pp. 15, 28, 76, 77, 78, 81, 95 (upper left and lower right), 96, 97, 98, 99, 102 courtesy of the author; pp. 28, 92, 95 (center and upper right), 100, 101, and 104 (right) taken at Gwynne's Greenhouse in Lyons, Colorado, courtesy of the author.

For everyone who has experienced the loss of a dear animal companion…
and especially those who feel alone in their grief

In loving memory of *Cleo, Sidney, Harmony, Bailey,* and *Bentley*

Near this spot are deposited the remains of one who possessed Beauty without Vanity, Strength without Insolence, Courage without Ferocity, and all the Virtues of Man without his Vices. This praise, which would be unmeaning Flattery if inscribed over human ashes, is but a just Tribute to the Memory of BOTSWAIN, a Dog.

—John Carn Hobhouse

CONTENTS

FOREWORD

The loss of a beloved pet can be a profound experience for many people. Recovering from the bereavement usually takes a lot of time and tears. Counselors who specialize in this field have always recognized that there are some activities that will help the bereaved owner. In the past I have recommended that, if possible, one should plant something as a living memorial. But until I read this book, I never really considered the creation of entire pet memory garden. And now I realize how much more effective and beautiful this would be.

One of the most successful prescriptions I give for self-help is continued daily activity. Getting involved in a creative and challenging project is even better therapy. The creation of a special garden in memory of a deceased pet or pets is one of the most

Every blade of grass has its angel that bends over it and whispers, "Grow, grow."

The Talmud

creative and productive things any pet lover can do. Aside from the wonderful therapy this provides, it will also create a permanent loving memorial. But it is a living memorial as well. Gardens need constant tending, and they grow and change in their own unique ways. This is suggestive of the beloved pets we have known and lost. And the actual physical work becomes a labor of love and remembrance. We become involved in the creation of something alive and beautiful that did not exist before. What a marvelous embodiment this is of what a memorial should be!

Going back to nature, we can find beauties and healings we don't usually experience in our "normal" daily lives. A garden can become an emotional and spiritual oasis—a place of serenity and personal reflection and loving memory. How wonderful it must be to have this in one's own backyard, always there beckoning to us.

Whether you have the space and time to create an entire garden or just put in a tree or single plant, this book can help you. As the author indicates, the psychological significance of a garden symbolizes a compassionate heart ready to bloom again. It is a welcoming back and a reverence for life. Of course, the best memorial is in one's own heart. But any kind of special garden setting is one of the most wonderful possible places to enhance one's inner memorial. This book offers an undertaking that would be a unique tribute, creating a very personal beautiful physical refuge with a unique aura of peace and remembrance.

Wallace Sife, Ph.D.
Author of *The Loss of a Pet* and founder/president of the Association for Pet Loss and Bereavement

PREFACE

Those mourning the loss of a pet often express similar feelings. Many talk about how special their relationship with their pet was—a relationship they say is difficult, if not impossible, to describe to others. They were connected with their pet in a way they have rarely been connected with any other living creature, even a human being. There was an otherworldly ease to the relationship, as if this animal were their soul mate.

Many also complain that no one understands or appreciates their grief. Frequently they are downright angry that their friends and loved ones dismiss or minimize their loss. While it is human nature to hope that others can feel what is in our heart, we make our own pain worse when we let other people's reactions cause us distress. The reason people don't understand the loss of a pet is

All suffering prepares the soul for vision.

Martin Buber

because they have not experienced a similar bond. Someday, if they are very lucky, they may come to know why people like you and I are so affected by the loss of a beloved pet.

As you think about creating a garden in memory of your pet, there is something important for you to know. It is possible not only to recover from grief and loss, but to rise from its painful depths to a place of profound peace and acceptance with a completely new commitment to life and love.

Working through grief is a daunting journey. It requires courage, conviction, and the faith that light *will* shine on the other side of this dark path. There is no failure in not accepting the challenge grief presents, but to refuse it may diminish your capacity to experience the richness life still has to offer. When you turn from those wounds that are asking for healing, you also turn from that place within you that knows love, compassion, and peace.

At the beginning of your journey, you may feel reluctant to embrace the emotional challenge of grieving. During this time you need all the support you can get. Fortunately, support *is* available—the support of a comforting spiritual force in nature.

It is my hope that this book will help you find a sense of connection to the greater power that infuses all life and to experience a profound healing beyond that of just "getting back to normal." I also hope that you will find validation for what you already know: that what really matters never dies. The love you gave to your pet and the love your pet gave to you opened your heart in a very special way. This love, death cannot alter.

ACKNOWLEDGMENTS

I am sincerely grateful to those clients of mine who have shared with me their heartbreak over the loss of a pet. What I have learned from them is beyond measure.

I am grateful to the contributors to this book—kindred spirits who have found solace and comfort in nature. I have been amazed at the incredible memorials they have created in memory of their pets—living tributes to a bond that they could not always describe in words but could reflect in this beautiful form of living art. With great appreciation I acknowledge June Lynne Mucci, Marge Loyd, Sybil Allison Graham, Abigail Marie Coyour, Harrison Dunbar, Andrew Dominic Psyhos, Kathy Kromm, Elyn Zerfas, Aleta Hogan, Pam Horner, Shirley Norman, Diane Newman, Sandra Laemmle, Sandra S. Nelson, and Judith A. Ruta.

Bread feeds the body, indeed, but flowers feed also the soul.

The Koran

I thank Royce Dunbar and Brenda Olson Dunbar for their friendship and fantastic photography. I eagerly await their future projects.

Dr. Wallace Sife is warm-heartedly acknowledged for his work in the field of pet loss and bereavement. He has greatly raised awareness of the significance of pet loss in the counseling profession while offering helpful comfort to the bereaved.

Thanks to Michelle Raye for her unique stones that adorn so many memorial gardens and the exceptional comfort she offers to the bereaved.

Much appreciation to Ian Dunbar and Meredith Ver Steeg for their willingness to participate in this book.

I especially want to express my gratitude to my greatest teachers—Nicholas, Andrew and Christopher—for their love, support, and encouragement. It is through the laughs and challenges we have shared together that I have stretched and grown. My love for them knows no bounds.

NATURE'S HEALING SPIRIT

There is something unearthly, almost divine, in the bond we form with our pets. The animals we bring into our lives ask very little from us, yet they love us unconditionally. Without receiving an apology, they forgive us. Without judging, they accept us. One tender scratch behind the ears, and we have a friend for life. This is a relationship purely of the heart—a relationship that touches us deeply, almost too deeply to admit.

When a pet dies, the depth of this connection demands to be admitted. To fully heal, we must admit it. But this may not be easy in a culture that does not always appreciate or honor such relationships. Not everyone understands that the loss of a pet can trigger grief as deep and intense as the loss of a person. Not everyone understands that is all right to mourn the loss of an an animal.

All my hurts My garden spade can heal.

Ralph Waldo Emerson

Snookie

Snookie is buried next to the trunk of a pecan tree. I planted lavender phlox behind her headstone. The phlox is soft and gentle, like Snookie. A large stone angel holding a flower and a smaller angel watch over her. I keep pecans by her grave because she loved pecans, raw or baked.

Snookie was friendly to everyone and everything except squirrels. Whenever I spotted a squirrel around the pecan tree, I'd whisper loudly, "Snookie, there's a squirrel!" and off she would fly. She would have climbed that tree if she could have, she wanted the squirrel so badly. She'd run around the tree for a long time, sniffing the squirrels scent, nose to the ground, following its tracks. When I buried her, I told her through my tears that I would give her as many pecans as she wanted as long as she kept the squirrels away.

Snookie's death was very, very hard; she was so special. In many ways, pets are like children: you're responsible for them and take care of them. Thirteen years—we'd been through a lot together.

People do all kinds of things to ease their pain. I found working in the garden to be good therapy. Sometimes I'd stop working and cry, but I wanted to be near her, regardless of how much it hurt. Gardening kept me going.

There is a bit of God in every pet. They love us unconditionally, and from what I've been taught, that's the way God loves us, too. So, when we get close to a pet, we're getting closer to God. Gardens are sacred in this way, too, so to bury Snookie among the flowers seemed very natural and appropriate.

—June Lynne Mucci, Kannapolis, North Carolina

Grief evokes feelings of powerlessness, helplessness. We can do nothing to change what has happened to us. We miss what we've lost with all our being. We are paralyzed by frustration and pain.

This sense of helplessness can range from active rage to passive despair. It can be the darkest time of our life. When overcome with sorrow, our hearts tend to contract. It is an understandable, protective reflex, but this closing down diminishes our aliveness. Giving ourselves compassionate permission to mourn with an open heart is difficult; to embrace our pain makes us feel as though we will die—but we won't.

A wide variety of feelings can surface during the grieving process. Many people mistakenly believe that grief is only an emotion of sadness. While sadness may predominate, feelings of longing, guilt, and anger are common as well. You may even feel relief in some circumstances. All feelings are normal. All emotions can be resolved. Emotions are energy. When you do not allow your feelings to surface, the energy becomes trapped in your body. *What you resist will persist; what you feel, you will heal.* Consciously allowing your feelings to emerge, and experiencing them fully, puts you on the path to recovery. Sometimes, it helps to focus on just one feeling at a time. To single out, acknowledge, experience, and release even one emotion is difficult but worth the effort.

Many people wonder how long grieving will—or should—take. The only appropriate answer is ... until it is finished. Mourning is considered complete when the memory of what has been lost no longer evokes painful feelings of suffering and is instead replaced by a sense of acceptance. Some feelings of sadness and regret over the loss of a beloved pet may always be present.

But over time the feelings can shift from suffering in sorrow and pain to a bittersweet sense of gratitude and remembrance that evokes joy. An intimate relationship with the spiritual can take you far beyond mere acceptance of your loss; it will lead you to your innermost heart where you can find the peace that surpasses understanding, the love that knows no time, place, or conditions.

A recent loss can revive feelings from past losses, even when the grief caused by those previous losses was thought to have been resolved. When you feel bad, it is not always necessary to pinpoint the source of the pain. Understanding involves the logical mind, the intellect, but pain is transformed through emotional acceptance. This is where the natural world comes in.

When you connect with nature, you tap into the energy of love you once shared with your companion animal. This love is the balm your bruised heart needs when grieving. Nature sings a song that your heart can hear; it feeds your soul. It will, if you allow it, begin reengaging you in life. Because nature is always present, the key to connecting with it lies in relaxing, allowing, and accepting. You do not have to do a thing. Nature is available and open to all who seek it.

If you have recently lost a pet, you may be longing for a deep connection with something pure. With a subtle shift in perception, you can find such purity within yourself and in the tender, caring spirit of nature. Allow the natural world to hold you as you move through your grief. Let your heart lead you into the garden where you can be "hooked" back into life again.

Experiencing the subtle, loving energies of the natural world is unspeakably sweet. Too often, however, we take this natural

Dinkum Do

When I saw this amazing multi-colored parrot—a Sun Conure—at the pet shop, it was love at first sight. I decided his name would be Dinkum Do, or "Dinks" as we called him.

The average life span of parrots like Dinks is thirty years. Everyday I would say to him, "Thirty more years," or "Twenty-nine more years," and so on as time went by. He went everywhere we went—in the car, on camping trips. When I had to go to work, I would get up an hour early just so I could hold him. At night, he would fall asleep under my shirt right by my heart.

In the wintertime I would let him fly around the house a little since I was the only one home most of the time. He was an avid flyer, finding me in any room I went in.

One day when we had company over, he suddenly swooped out of the room. I heard someone in another room asking, "What's wrong with him?" I was afraid to look. There on the floor was this beautiful little bird lying with *his wings spread out. I picked him up and actually felt his soul leave his body. He just closed his eyes and in a flash was gone. I held him until my husband made me lay him in a box. I kept saying, "Maybe he is just stunned," but deep in my heart I knew he was gone. What was supposed to be thirty years turned out to be only four. We buried him with his favorite toy in my herb garden. I feel for everyone who loses a pet because they are such a big part of your life.*

—Marge Loyd, Pasadena, Maryland

world—and life in general—for granted. The death of a beloved pet can make us realize how precious life is. It can push us into contact with parts of our inner selves that we have never consciously touched before. Following this thread inward can lead, paradoxically, to a deeper connection with the world at large.

We are beginning to grow in our understanding of the reciprocal relationship we have with Mother Earth. As we wake up to the negative effects we have had on the earth, we can also open ourselves to the tremendous amount of strength and nurturing available in nature. And as we process our pain, we can enter into a new relationship with the earth that is ultimately healing for both the planet and ourselves. After all, it is from the earth's substances that our bodies are formed. This good mother feeds us, quenches our thirst, gives us air to breathe, and clothes and shelters us.

When I was in the depths of personal despair, I would walk for two miles every day through a nature preserve. At first, I walked at breakneck speed, only occasionally allowing my attention to wander to a flitting bird or noisy squirrel. The fast pace seemed to diffuse my body's painful energy of grief. Eventually, though, I slowed down and began to experience the purity and perfection of the natural beauty surrounding me. I began to feel a stirring deep in the core of my being. Slowly, I let down my guard against the grief I was feeling and accepted nature's gift of quiet, steady grace. This grace had been there all along; I had just been too absorbed to notice it. As my tension gradually unwound and I relaxed to the spiritual support of the natural world around me, I was gradually able to release my feelings of grief.

You, too, can open yourself to the natural spirit that enfolds and permeates life. You, too, can embrace the healing force of nature. One way to release your feelings of grief is by creating a garden of memory as a living tribute to your lost pet.

Many people intuitively seek refuge in gardening in times of sorrow. Gardening connects us directly with the cycle of life. A garden is itself a metaphor for life. (Life began in a garden, according to the Bible.) Gardens are vulnerable to the vagaries of climate and environment. They need loving care as they grow and mature. They experience vigorous periods of growth and bloom, punctuated by quiet periods of resting and renewing.

As you tend your memorial garden and watch it change through the seasons, you will see it maturing, becoming more beautiful as the plants become stronger, fuller, and more vibrant. You will see it reflecting your own healing and the beauty of your relationship with your beloved pet. In time, you will be rewarded with a more tender, compassionate heart that is ready to bloom ... and love ... again.

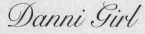

Danni Girl

I believe that dogs are sacred and are put on this earth as a gift from God to teach humans profound lessons about life, love, death, and spirituality. The spiritual connection we share with dogs is intense and unique. Such was the case with my dog, Danni, or "Danni Girl" as so many people called her.

Danni was a dog with spunk and compassion. She loved children and elderly people. Weekly we would visit nursing homes and hospitals as a part of Project Pup, a pet therapy program. Danni would place a tennis ball in a patient's lap or on the top of a bed. She brought a great deal of joy and happiness to many people. She listened intently as people talked to her and always knew the right time to give a kiss.

When Danni was three, she developed a rare auto-immune disease. If not reversed, the disease could kill her. It was made clear to me that a rough road lay ahead and that there were no guarantees. Treatment would be costly, but, if necessary, I was prepared to get a second mortgage on my house. I would do whatever it took to treat Danni—as long as she kept fighting and her pain was controlled. There was another, less selfish reason to proceed with the treatment. Because the condition was rare in dogs, Danni was providing valuable information for veterinary science that might be beneficial to other dogs with the same condition.

While undergoing treatment, Danni practically lived at the veterinary hospital. I made the forty-minute trip twice daily to visit with her, and she gradually began to get better. The final step in her treatment plan involved surgery to remove parts of her lung and bladder. Because there was a risk that Danni might die in surgery, I second-guessed my decision to move ahead, but I concluded that since we had come this far, we had to continue. But I decided that this was the last medical treatment I would put Danni through; it was just too stressful for her. The morning of the surgery, I sat by the phone waiting for the surgeon to call. Every time the phone rang, I jumped with anticipation and fear. Finally, after four hours, the call came. With exhaustion and relief in her voice, the surgeon informed me that everything had gone smoothly and Danni was in recovery. Words can't adequately describe the mixture of emotions I felt.

During her recuperation, Danni received cards, toys, and homemade chicken soup from friends, neighbors, and nursing home patients. I was touched *that so many people loved and supported her. As if making up for lost time, Danni began to act like a puppy again. Soon she was back visiting patients.*

Years later, about six months before her thirteenth birthday, Danni suffered a grand mal seizure. In my heart I knew that this was the beginning of the end for Danni. Her seizures increased from a few times a day to several times an hour. Medication did not help. The thought of putting her through the stress of elaborate medical testing tortured me. The thought of not doing so also tortured me. One morning, after a sleepless night that had exhausted both of us, I began to cry and Danni moved close to me. She put her head next to mine and licked my tears. Then she stared at me with a stare that went right through me. I knew what I had to do, and it was the hardest decision I had ever made in my life. I called my veterinarian and, with a cracking voice, told her that I was bringing Danni in. On the way to the hospital, Danni, for the first time ever, did not ride with her head out of the car window. When we arrived at the hospital, staff members led us to one of the examining rooms and put a bedspread on the floor for all of us to sit on. Then they explained the procedure. After the first of two injections was administered, I stroked Danni and talked to her until she fell unconscious. I could not stay for the rest; the pain was far too great. All of the staff members were crying. They loved Danni and knew what she had had to endure.

Danni died a week before her thirteenth birthday. In her honor, I planted a crab apple tree in the backyard and surrounded it with a small perennial garden. I chose crab apple because Danni loved to lie under flowering trees and take in their aromas. The garden is located alongside the pool and the part of the yard in which Danni would play fetch with a tennis ball. I also got a nameplate for a bench on my deck that says "In Loving Memory of Danni Girl." When I sit on this bench, I can still hear Danni's bark and see the flash of her white, curly fur as she leaps into the pool after a tennis ball.

Time does heal pain, but it took a very long time for me to feel better. I joined a pet bereavement support group, read books on pet loss, and tried to avoid the people who said stupid things like: "She was just a dog. It's not as if a human being died." My comfort comes from my memories of her and the stories I tell about her. I miss her and think about her every day, and I feel her spirit around me all the time. Danni and I share an eternal spiritual connection. She was a gift to me and to all those she touched.

—Sybil Allison Graham, Bloomfield, Connecticut

2
CHILDREN AND PET LOSS

For many children, losing a pet is their introduction to death and loss. While they may not show it overtly or be able to articulate it, they are often deeply affected by such loss. The death of a pet is an opportunity not only to help children cope with their immediate grief, but to give them tools for coping with future losses.

The first thing to do in helping children cope with pet loss is to acknowledge the deep connection they had with their pet. Let them know that you understand that they have lost a very close, very important friend.

Children have a propensity to fantasize. Be gentle and listen respectfully as you discuss the pet's death with them, but honestly confront any unrealistic illusions they may have. Reassure them that the pet's death was not their fault, that there was nothing they

He who plants a garden plants happiness.

Chinese proverb

Coal

After my family and I saw a miniature horse at the Minnesota State Fair, I decided that I had to have one of my own. When I had raised a enough money to buy one, my mom and dad took me to a farm in Menominee, Wisconsin. We looked at dozens of miniature horses, and in the last bunch I found the one I liked. It was like love at first sight! Her paper name was Coal Little Char; I called her Coal for short. She was black with brown tints here and there, about thirty-two inches high, and very round— she was going to have a baby!

Coal's baby turned out to be a girl. I brought Coal and Fudge to every parade I could. The people just loved them. I also took them to county fairs. There was no special class for miniature horses, so I had to show Coal against the big horses. I would wake up early the morning of the show and wash Coal and spray her down (which she hated) to make her all pretty and shiny. I would also polish her hooves and comb her hair. It surprised me when Coal would win second and third places against the big horses, but I knew she deserved it.

One Sunday morning after church, I was putting flowers in a vase and thinking about how the pastor had said that flowers represent life and a new beginning when my father walked slowly into the house. He didn't look at all happy. "Abby," he said, "I'm sorry, but Coal has passed away." I did not want to believe him. Finally I got the courage to go out and see her for myself. As I got close to Coal, I started crying, "I'm sorry, I'm sorry."

We never knew for sure what caused Coal to die. In her memory, I put a stone in the garden in front of our house.

—Abigail Marie Coyour, Frederic, Wisconsin

could have done to change the outcome and nothing they can do now to bring the pet back. It is very common for children to feel guilt for what has happened.

Be prepared for a range of emotions and behaviors during this time, keeping in mind that children do not express themselves in the same ways as adults. Sleep, appetite, concentration, energy levels may all be affected. Children may have more difficulty getting along with others. They may be clingier, or want more time alone. Understand that these are the normal symptoms of grieving.

Offer children an open, healthy model of grieving. Trying to protect children by concealing honest emotions can boomerang. Children may feel betrayed, abandoned, or resentful if they perceive that you are untouched by the loss. Let children know that you are hurting, too, while explaining that everyone grieves in their own way.

The death of a pet can also be a good opportunity to speak openly with children about spiritual beliefs. Death always has a way of asking us to take a deeper, more meaningful look at life.

Affirm and normalize what children are feeling, particularly feelings of anger. Expressions of anger can range from quiet withdrawal to violent acting-out. Try to help children manage this anger. Let them know that, while it is normal to be mad, being mad is never an excuse to hurt oneself or others. Provide safe outlets for negative energy. Some children may find release in creative activities, such as drawing or working with clay. Others may find physical exertion a more effective release of angry feelings.

Reassure children that their pain will eventually go away. It is hard for anyone to keep perspective when they are grieving, but it is especially hard for children. I do not recommend immediately going out and buying a new pet to replace the one that has died. Let some time pass first. You will know when the time is right to bring a new pet into the house.

Involve the children in planning a memorial ceremony for the pet. A good time for such a ceremony would be when the animal is buried or its ashes scattered. A memorial ceremony can help bring closure and acceptance not only for children but for anyone who was close to the animal. See chapter seven for ideas for remembrance rituals.

Finally, encourage children to memorialize their pet. There are many ways to do this: photo albums, collages, memory books. But there is no better way to memorialize a pet than by creating a memory garden in the pet's honor. When you make a garden, nature adds its own unique healing spirit to the grieving process. Making a garden is a wonderful way to spend time with children and help them work through their feelings of loss. Once completed, and for years to follow, the garden will be a place the children can tend and remember the love they shared with their precious animal.

Lily came to live with us when I was two years old and she was a kitten. I would hold her upside down and she didn't mind. Sometimes I would put her in my stroller and push her around.

When I was three, Lily had five kittens. She was a good mom. She always wanted to protect the kitties and I wanted to play with them.

She liked to sleep with me every night because I think she thought I was one of her kittens.

We lived together until I was eight. She died on a hot July night. I was very sad and didn't want to give up hope that she might not really be dead. We searched for her all over our neighborhood. We searched for her at the animal shelter and at the pound. The people at the pound said they had found a body of a cat just like Lily on the street in front of our house.

My friends didn't really understand why I was so sad. Later my Uncle Peter bought me a book called Cat Heaven. I cried every time I read that book, but it helped me realize that she was in a better place.

We have a stone with her name on it and a cat statue next to some cat-mint in our garden. It helps me remember how much she liked to be outside.

Even though we don't have Lily anymore, we do have one of her kittens and that helps. Sometimes, I talk with him about his mom, and he seems to understand. He must miss her, too.

—Harrison Dunbar, Des Moines, Iowa

Bailey

I remember when we first got Bailey. She was a cute little silver puppy that everyone instantly fell in love with. What set Bailey apart from other dogs was her loving personality. If you got down on your knees, she'd come up and stand on her hind legs and actually give you a kind of doggie hug. She knew when you were feeling down, and she'd slowly come up to you and just cuddle, making you feel much better.

Not only was she the perfect dog to relax with, she had an amazing energetic spirit. Bailey loved to participate in the family activities. When we went sledding, she'd be right there, chasing us down the hill or jumping on for a ride. She also loved the river that ran our property. One of my favorite things to do in the summer was to go tubing with my brothers. And of course, Bailey would be right there with us.

Bailey was the greatest dog. I miss her.

—Andrew Dominic Psyhos, Lyons, Colorado

3

GIVING YOUR GARDEN MEANING

When a beloved pet dies, life can feel as if it has slipped into chaos. The comfortable, normal routines of everyday living are shaken. You find yourself searching for meaning and understanding of what has happened. You seek answers that are not easily found.

As hard as it is to believe, however, the sun can shine again. Gardening can connect you with nature, engage your creativity, provide a physical outlet, and satisfy the psychological need for ritual to memorialize your pet. If your pet was cremated, it can be consoling and reassuring to scatter the ashes in your own garden.

Dedicating a space in your yard or on your patio to plant a perennial garden allows you to memorialize this special animal through the loving language of flowers and plants. You can welcome the essence of life back into your world. Setting up a

More things grow in the garden than the gardener sows.

Spanish proverb

T.J. Flopp

T.J. Flopp was a silver mini lop. We took his name came from a book by Stephen Cosgrove that my husband, Marshall, gave me on our anniversary. The name seemed perfect because in the book "T.J." stood for "thoroughly joyful."

Four years after we got T.J., Marshall was diagnosed with cancer. Throughout the treatment, T.J. was his constant companion. After Marshall died, a kind hospital chaplain pointed out that T.J., like the rest of us, would feel his absence and suggested that I give T.J. some of Marshall's clothes to help ease the loss. T.J.'s silent presence was a great gift during this period of grieving.

My garden has always been where I go in times of difficulty. Marshall's memory garden grew and gave me constant comfort, even though there were days when I watered it only with my tears.

When T.J. was ten, the vet told me that his aging body would not be able to hang on much longer. I prepared for T.J.'s transition by reading the same words to him that I read to Marshall when he was dying: "You will never know how grateful I am for your presence in my life, and I am honored by the privilege of knowing you and being here with you." I found a kind vet who would come to the house. After the euthanasia, I wrapped T.J.'s body in one of Marshall's shirts.

The next morning, there was a single bud on Marshall's memory rose, a "Grand Marshall." It was the only rose in the whole garden that morning. I knew it was Marshall's way of telling me that I had done the right thing.

I chose a wonderful red rose called "Braveheart" as a memory flower for T.J. I put T.J.'s cage near Marshall's memory garden, and on the top of the cage I placed a planter of "million bells"—since every time a bell rings an angel gets his wings. In addition to "bunny tails," the garden contains clover, which T.J. loved and which in flower-language means "think of me."

—Kathy Kromm, Portland, Oregon

birdbath, birdhouse, or feeder and welcoming butterflies with colorful plant blooms are further invitations to life by sharing yourself and giving back to nature.

For thousands of years, the symbolism of plants has played a significant role in human history. The Bible has references to plants; Shakespeare spoke of herbs and flowers; and the Victorians expressed what was in their hearts through flowers.

When you create a garden in remembrance, you let plants and flowers express what is in *your* heart. Through their unique language, you can symbolically honor and remember the special pet who shared your life and love.

*Y*ou don't have to have a large space to create a living memorial to a pet. For those without the room or the ability to create an elaborate, in-ground garden, a patio or indoor pot can be planted instead. A simple potted planting can be just as meaningful as a more complex garden. Here's one suggestion: Bend a wire coat hanger into the shape of a heart, straighten the curved hook, and secure it in the potting soil. Then plant a climbing vine that you can train to grow up the wire. **Rosemary** (symbolizing *remembrance*), **English ivy** (symbolizing *friendship*), and **creeping fig** are some of the easiest and most popular plants to train into a topiary form.

Plants Representing Each Month

Choose from this list to symbolize a birthday or anniversary month.

January	carnation; snowdrop
February	violet; primrose
March	daffodil; violet
April	daisy
May	lily-of-the-valley
June	rose
July	larkspur; water lily; sweet pea
August	gladiolus
September	aster
October	calendula; dahlia
November	chrysanthemum
December	holly; poinsettia

Raby

Losing Raby, my twelve-year-old Abyssinian cat, to cancer was devastating. Over time, I have learned that accepting the reality of the loss, instead of resisting it, allows me to honor his life and our relationship. The pain has lessened, even though I once thought it never would.

I have memorialized Raby's life and his passing in many ways. From the time I first found out he was sick until he died, I carried a small pouch that held Native American symbols of a safe journey. I kept the pouch close to me and believed it would be a way for my spirit to be with him always. At his memorial service in the park next to the local humane society, where he rests, I placed the pouch beside the box I'd made for his ashes. At that service, I said the following:

"Raby, you came into my life twelve years ago and found a home in my heart. I know we'll be together again, because our bond was too strong for the few short years given us. The void you leave in this life is

a mixture of unbearable pain and tears of joy as I remember your antics, your beauty, your intelligence, and your unconditional love."

A series of spiritual events preceded my knowledge of Raby's illness. I didn't know anything was wrong with him, but I began to say that I was afraid of loving him too much. I was afraid, but had no idea why. Once, when I was holding him in my arms, I felt a connection between us that I had never felt before and cannot explain to this day. It can best be described as a silent bonding of souls. I was elated but unnerved by the experience. I called my partner, Marti, to try to explain, but there were no words for the feeling.

One night I awoke suddenly with the word "cancer" rattling through my brain. I looked and saw Raby sleeping peacefully by my side. Shortly afterwards Raby began to cough. Then it became apparent that he was losing weight. The veterinarian confirmed my worst fear… Raby had cancer.

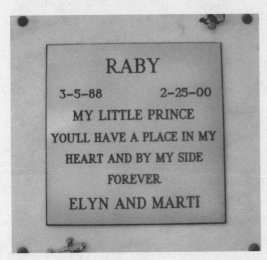

Other pets may follow, but no animals ever replace the ones you have loved and lost. Nor should they.

—Elyn Zerfas
Fort Lauderdale, Florida

The Symbolism of Color

Using the language of colors in your garden, you can further reflect your loved one's personality.

White
purity and love

Yellow
intellect, optimism, good humor, wisdom

Orange
joy, confidence, independence, sociableness

Purple
intuition, idealism, self-sacrifice, inspiration, kindness, spirituality

Green
generosity, understanding, healing, humility, compassion

Red
passion, courage, spontaneity, strength, love

Blue
loyalty, affection, tranquility, patience

The Victorian Language of Flowers

The Victorians used plants to create a special language. You can use this language to add further meaning to your memory garden.

A

acacia: friendship
acacia, pink or white: elegance
acacia, yellow: secret love
acanthus: the fine arts; artifice
achillea millefolium (yarrow): war
aconite (wolfsbane; monkshood): misanthropy
adonis: painful recollections
agrimony: thankfulness; gratitude
allspice: compassion
almond: stupidity; indiscretion
almond blossom: hope
aloe: grief
alyssum: worth beyond beauty
amaranth, globe: immortality; unfading love
amaryllis: pride; timidity; splendid beauty
American cowslip: divine beauty; "You are my divinity."
American elm: patriotism
American linden: matrimony
American starwort: welcome to a stranger; cheerfulness in old age
amethyst (browallia): admiration
anemone: sickness; expectation; forsaken
angelica: inspiration
apple: temptation

apple, thorn: deceitful charms

apple blossom: preference; "Fame speaks him great and good."

apricot blossom: doubt

arborvitae: unchanging friendship; "Live for me."

arum: ardor; zeal

ash tree: grandeur

aspen tree: lamentation

asphodel: "My regrets follow you to the grave."

aster, China: variety; afterthought

auricula: painting; "Entreat me not."

auricula, scarlet: avarice

azalea: first love; temperance

baby's breath: everlasting love

bachelor's-button: celibacy

balm: sympathy; pleasantry

Balm of Gilead: cure; relief

balsam: impatience

balsam, red: "Do not touch me."

barberry: sharpness; sourness of temper

basil: hatred

basket-of-gold: calm; reconciliation

bay leaf: "I change but in death."

bay tree: glory

bay wreath: reward

bee balm: compassion; sympathy; consolation

bee orchis: industry

beech tree: prosperity

begonia: dark thoughts

belladona: silence

bellflower, pyramidal: constancy

bellflower, small white: gratitude

betony: surprise

bindweed, great: insinuation

bindweed, small: humility

birch: meekness

bittersweet nightshade: truth

black poplar: courage

blackthorn: difficulty

bladder nut tree: frivolity; amusement

blue-flowered Greek valerian: rupture

bluebell: constancy

blueberry: treachery

borage: bluntness

boxwood: stoicism

bramble: envy

branch of currants: "You please all."

branch of thorns: severity; rigor

bridal rose: happy love

broom: humility; neatness

browallia (amethyst): admiration

buckbean: calm repose

bud of white rose: heart ignorant of love

bugloss: falsehood

bulrush: indiscretion; docility

bundle of reeds: music; complaisance

burdock: importunity; "Touch me not."

buttercup: ingratitude; childishness; desire for riches

butterfly orchis: gaiety

butterfly weed: "Let me go."

cabbage: profit

cactus: warmth

camellia, red: excellence

camellia, white: loveliness

campanula: gratitude

canary grass: perseverance

candytuft: indifference

canterbury bell: acknowledgment

Cape jasmine: transport of joy; "I am too happy."

cardinal flower: distinction

carnation, pink: woman's love

carnation, red: "Alas for my poor heart."

carnation, striped: refusal

carnation, yellow: disdain

catchfly: snare

catchfly, red: youthful love

catchfly, white: betrayed

cedar: strength

cedar leaf: "I live for thee."

cedar of Lebanon: incorruptible

celandine, lesser: joys to come

centaury: delicacy

cereus: modest genius; horror

chamomile: energy in adversity

checkered fritillary: persecution

cherry blossom: good education

cherry tree, white: deception

chervil: sincerity

chestnut tree: luxury; "Do me justice."

chickweed: rendezvous

chicory: frugality

China aster: variety

China aster, double: "I share your sentiments."

China aster, single: "I will think of it."

China or Indian pink: aversion

China rose: beauty always new

Chinese chrysanthemum: cheerfulness under adversity

Chinese lantern plant (winter cherry): deception

Christmas rose: "Relieve my anxiety."

chrysanthemum, red: love

chrysanthemum, white: truth

chrysanthemum, yellow: slighted love

cilantro (coriander): hidden worth

cinquefoil: maternal affection

cistus (rockrose): popular favor

cistus, gum: "I shall die tomorrow."

citron: ill-natured beauty

clematis: mental beauty; "I love your mind."

clematis, evergreen: poverty

clover, four-leaved: "Be mine."

clover, red: industry

clover, white: "Think of me."

cloves: dignity

cobaea: gossip

colchicum: "My best days are past."

coltsfoot: "Justice shall be done."

columbine: folly

columbine, purple: resolved to win

columbine, red: anxious and trembling

convolvulus: bonds; uncertainty

convolvulus, major: extinguished hopes

convolvulus, minor: repose; night

convolvulus, pink: worth sustained by judicious and tender affection

coreopsis: always cheerful

coreopsis Arkansa: love at first sight

coriander (cilantro): hidden worth

corn: riches

corn bottle: delicacy

corn cockle: gentility

cornel tree: duration

cornflower: healing; felicity; delicacy

coronilla (crown vetch): "Success crown your wishes."

cowslip: pensiveness; winning grace

cowslip, American: divine beauty; "You are divine."

cranberry: cure for heartache; hardness

crape myrtle: eloquence

creeping cereus: modest genius; horror

cress: stability; power

crocus: abuse not

crocus, saffron: mirth

crocus, spring: youthful gladness

crowfoot: ingratitude; luster

crowsbill: envy

cudweed, American: unceasing remembrance

currant: "Thy frown will kill me."

cyclamen: diffidence

cypress: death; mourning; despair

daffodil: regard

daffodil, yellow: chivalry

dahlia: instability

daisy: innocence; "I share your sentiments."

daisy, Michaelmas: farewell; afterthought

daisy, parti-colored: beauty

daisy, wild: "I will think of it."

damask rose: brilliant complexion; freshness

dandelion: oracle

daphne: glory; immortality

daphne odora: painting the lily

darnel (rye grass): vice; changeable disposition

day lily: coquetry

dead leaves: sadness

dianthus: pure love

dianthus, red or pink: lively and pure affection

dittany of Crete: birth

dittany of Crete, white: passion

dock: patience

dogwood: durability

dried flax: utility

ebony tree: blackness

E

elder: zealousness
elm: dignity
endive: frugality
evergreen clematis: poverty
evergreen thorn: solace in adversity
everlasting: unceasing remembrance
everlasting pea: lasting pleasure

F

fennel: worthy of all praise; strength
fern: fascination
fig: argument
fig marigold: idleness
fig tree: prolific
filbert: reconciliation
fir: time
fir, Scotch: elevation
fireweed: pretension
flax: appreciation; domestic industry; fate; "I feel your kindness."
fleur-de-lis: flame; "I burn."
flowering fern: revery
flowering reed: confidence in heaven
fly orchis: error
fool's parsley: silliness
forget-me-not: true love; "Forget me not."
foxglove: insincerity
foxtail grass: insincerity
French honeysuckle: rustic beauty
French marigold: jealousy
French willow: bravery and humanity

G

fuchsia, scarlet: taste
Fuller's teasel: misanthropy
fumitory: spleen
furze: love for all seasons
gardenia: refinement
garland of roses: reward of virtue
gentian: "You are unjust."
geranium: gentility
geranium, dark: melancholy
geranium, ivy: bridal favor
geranium, lemon: unexpected meeting
geranium, nutmeg: expected meeting
geranium, oak-leaved: true friendship
geranium, penciled: ingenuity
geranium, scarlet: comforting; stupidity
geranium, scented: preference
geranium, silver-leaved: recall
geranium, wild: steadfast piety
germander speedwell: facility
gillyflower: bonds of affection
gladiolus: ready armed; strength of character
globe amaranth: unfading love; immortality
goat's rue: reason
goldenrod: precaution; encouragement
goldilocks: tardiness
gooseberry: anticipation
gorse: anger
gourd: extent; bulkiness

grape, wild: charity

grass: submission; utility

Guelder rose: winter; age

harebell: submission; grief

hawkweed: quick-sightedness

hawthorne: hope

hazel: reconciliation

heath: solitude

helenium: tears

heliotrope: accommodating disposition; devotion; faithfulness

hellebore: scandal; calumny

hemlock: "You will be my death."

hemp: fate

henbane: imperfection

hepatica: confidence

hibiscus: delicate beauty

holly: foresight

hollyhock: ambition; fecundity

honesty: honesty; fascination

honeysuckle: generous and devoted affection; bonds of love; sweetness of disposition

honeysuckle, coral: the color of my fate

honeysuckle, French: rustic beauty

hop: injustice

hornbeam: ornament

hortensia: "You are cold."

houseleek: vivacity; domestic industry

houstonia: content

hoya: sculpture

hundred-leaved rose: dignity of mind; pride; grace

hyacinth: sport; game; play

hyacinth, purple: sorrow

hyacinth, white: unobtrusive loveliness

hydrangea: a boaster; heartlessness

hyssop: cleanliness

ice plant: "Your looks freeze me."

Iceland moss: health

Indian Jasmine: attachment; "I attach myself to you."

Indian pink, double: always lovely

Indian plum: privation

iris: message

iris, German: flame

iris, yellow: flame of love

ivy: friendship; fidelity; marriage; faithful love; constancy

ivy, sprig of: assiduous to please

Jacob's ladder: "Come down."

Japan rose: "Beauty is your only attraction."

Japanese pear: fairies' fire

jasmine: amiability

jasmine, Cape: transport of love; "I am too happy."

jasmine, Carolina: separation

jasmine, Indian: attachment; "I attach myself to you."

jasmine, Spanish: sensuality

jasmine, yellow: grace and elegance

johnny-jump-up: happy thoughts

jonquil: "Return my affection."

Judas tree: unbelief; betrayal
juniper: succor; protection
kingcup: desire for riches; ingratitude; childishness
laburnum: forsaken; pensive beauty
lady's slipper: capriciousness; "Win me and wear me."
lagerstroemia, Indian (crape myrtle): eloquence
lamb's-ears: gentleness
lantana: rigor
larch: audacity; boldness
larkspur: lightness; levity
larkspur, pink: fickleness
larkspur, purple: haughtiness
laurel: glory
laurel, common (in flower): perfidy
laurel, ground: perseverance
laurel, mountain: ambition
lavender: distrust
leaves, dead: sadness
lemon: zest
lemon balm: sympathy, pleasantry
lemon blossom: fidelity in love
lettuce: coldheartedness
lichen: dejection; solitude
licorice, wild: "I declare against you."
lilac, field: humility
lilac, purple: first love
lilac, white: youthful innocence; youth
lily, day: coquetry

lily, imperial: majesty

lily, white: purity; sweetness; modesty; beauty

lily, yellow: falsehood; gaiety

lily-of-the-valley: return of happiness

linden or lime tree: conjugal love

live oak: liberty

liverwort: confidence

lobelia: malevolence

locust tree: affection beyond the grave; natural change

London pride: frivolity

lotus: eloquence

lotus flower: estranged love

love-in-a-mist: perplexity

love-lies-bleeding: hopeless, not heartless

lupine: voraciousness; imagination; sorrow

lychnis: wit

madder: calumny

magnolia: dignity; love of nature

magnolia, swamp: perseverance

mallow: mildness

mallow, marsh: beneficence

mallow, Syrian: consumed by love; persuasion

mallow, Venetian: delicate beauty

manchineel tree: falsehood

mandrake: horror

maple: reserve

marigold: grief; despair; uneasiness

marigold, African: vulgar minds

marigold, French: jealousy

marigold, prophetic: prediction

marjoram: blushes

meadow saffron: "My happiest days are past."

meadowsweet: uselessness

mercury: goodness

mesembryanthemum: idleness

mezereon: desire to please

Michaelmas daisy: afterthought; farewell

mignonette: "Your qualities surpass your charms."

milfoil: war

milkvetch: "You comfort me."

milkwort: hermitage

mimosa: sensitiveness

mint: virtue

mistletoe: "I surmount difficulties."

mock orange: counterfeit; memory

monkshood: chivalry; misanthropy

moonwort: forgetfulness

morning glory: affection; bond

moschatel: weakness

moss: maternal love

mosses: ennui

mossy saxifrage: affection

motherwort: concealed love

mountain ash: prudence

mouse-ear chickweed: ingenuous simplicity

mugwort: happiness

mulberry tree, black: "I shall not survive you."

mulberry tree, white: wisdom

mushroom: suspicion

mustard seed: indifference

myrobalan: privation

myrrh: gladness

myrtle: love

narcissus: egotism

nasturtium: patriotism

nemophila: "I forgive you."

nettle: slander; "You are cruel."

nettle tree: concert

night convolvulus: night

night-blooming cereus: transient beauty

nightshade: truth; silence

oak, white: independence

oak leaves: bravery

oak tree: hospitality

oats: the witching soul of music

oleander: "Beware."

olive tree: peace

orange blossom: chastity; bridal festivities

orange tree: generosity

orchid: thoughts

oregano: joy

osier: frankness

osmunda: dreams

ox eye: patience

N

O

P

palm: victory

pansy: (loving) thoughts

parsley: festivity

pasque flower: "You have no claims."

passion flower: faith

pea, everlasting: an appointed meeting; lasting pleasure

pea, sweet: departure; delicate pleasures

peach: "Your qualities, like your charms, are unequalled."

peach blossom: "I am your captive."

pear blossom: affection

pearly everlasting: never ceasing remembrance

pelargonium: eagerness

pennyroyal: "Flee away."

peony: shame; bashfulness

peppermint: warmth of feeling

periwinkle, blue: early friendship

periwinkle, white: pleasant memories

persimmon: "Bury me amid nature's beauties."

Peruvian heliotrope: devotion

petunia: "Your presence soothes me"; "Never despair."

phlox: unanimity; agreement

pimpernel: change

pine: pity

pine, pitch: philosophy

pink: boldness

pink, carnation: woman's love

pink, double Indian: always lovely

pink, double red: pure and ardent love

pink, mountain: aspiring
pink, single Indian: aversion
pink, single red: pure love
pink, variegated: refusal
pink, white: ingeniousness; talent
plane tree: genius
plum, Indian: privation
plum tree: fidelity
plum tree, wild: independence
polyanthus: pride of riches
polyanthus, crimson: the heart's mystery
polyanthus, lilac: confidence
pomegranate: foolishness
pomegranate flower: elegance
poplar, black: courage
poplar, white: time
poppy, oriental: silence
poppy, red: consolation
poppy, scarlet: extravagance
poppy, white: sleep
potato: benevolence
prickly pear: satire
primrose: youth; diffidence
primrose, evening: inconstancy
primrose, red: unpatronized merit
privet: prohibition
purple clover: provident
quaking grass: agitation

quince: temptation
ragged robin: wit
ranunculus: "You are radiant with charms and rich in attractions."
ranunculus, garden: "You are rich in attractions."
ranunculus, wild: ingratitude
raspberry: remorse
red catchfly: youthful love
red dianthus: lively and pure affection
red salvia: energy and esteem
reed, split: indiscretion
reeds, bundle of: music; amiability
rhododendrum, rosebay: danger; beware
rhubarb: advice
rocket: rivalry
rockrose (cistus): popular favor
rose: love
rose, Austrian: "Thou art all that is lovely."
rose, bridal: happy love
rose, burgundy: unconscious beauty
rose, cabbage: ambassador of love
rose, Carolina: "Love is dangerous."
rose, champion: "Only deserve my love."
rose, China: beauty always new
rose, Christmas: "Soothe my anxiety."
rose, daily: "Thy smile I aspire to."
rose, damask: brilliant complexion; freshness
rose, dog: pleasure and pain
rose, Guelder: winter; age

rose, hundred-leaved: pride; dignity of mind; grace

rose, Japan: "Beauty is your only attraction."

rose, La France: "Meet me by moonlight."

rose, maiden blush: "If you love me, you will find it out."

rose, multiflora: grace

rose, mundi: variety

rose, musk: capricious beauty

rose, musk (cluster): charming

rose, nephitos: infatuation

rose, red: bashful shame

rose, rock: popular favor

rose, single: simplicity

rose, thornless: early attachment

rose, unique: "Call me not beautiful."

rose, white: spiritual love; purity; "I am worthy of you."

rose, white (withered): transient impressions

rose, yellow: decrease of love; jealousy

rose, York and Lancaster: war

rosebay rhododendron: beware; danger

rosebud, moss: confession of love

rosebud, red: pure and lovely

rosebud, white: girlhood

rosemary: devotion; remembrance

roses, crown of: reward of virtue

roses (red and white together): unity

rudbeckia: justice

rue: disdain

rush: docility

_S_

rye grass (darnel): vice; changeable disposition

saffron: "Beware of excess."

saffron, crocus: mirth

saffron, meadow: "My happiest days are past."

sage: domestic virtue; esteem; good health

sainfoin: agitation

Saint John's wort: animosity; superstition

salvia, blue: thinking of you

salvia, red: energy and esteem; forever yours

saxifrage, mossy: affection

scabious: unfortunate love

scabious, sweet: widowhood

scarlet lychnis: sunbeaming eyes

scotch fir: elevation

sea thrift: sympathy

sensitive plant: sensibility; delicate feelings

shamrock: lightheartedness

shepherd's purse: "I offer you my all."

snapdragon: presumption

snowball: bound

snowdrop: hope

sorrel: affection

sorrel, wild: wit ill-timed

sorrel, wood: joy; maternal tenderness

southernwood: jest; bantering

Spanish jasmine: sensuality

spearmint: warmth of sentiment

speedwell: fidelity

speedwell, Germander: facility

speedwell, spiked: semblance

spiderwort: esteem not love

spindle tree: "Your charms are engraved on my heart."

spruce: hope in adversity; farewell

Star of Bethlehem: purity

starwort: afterthought

starwort, American: cheerfulness in old age; welcome to a stranger

stock: lasting beauty

stock, ten-week: promptness

stonecrop: tranquility

straw: agreement

straw, broken: quarrel; rupture of a contract

straw, whole: union

strawberry blossom: foresight

strawberry tree: esteem and love

sumac, Venice: splendor; intellectual excellence

sunflower, dwarf: adoration

sunflower, tall: haughtiness

swallowwort: cure for heartache

sweet basil: good wishes

sweet pea: delicate pleasures; departure

sweet sultan: felicity

sweet william: gallantry

sweetbrier, American: simplicity

sweetbrier, European: poetry; "I wound to heal."

sweetbrier, yellow: decrease of love

syringa: memory

syringa, Carolina: disappointment
tamarisk: crime
tansy, wild: "I declare war against you."
Teasel, Fuller's: misanthropy
thistle, common: austerity
thistle, Scotch: retaliation
thorn, apple: deceitful charms
thorns, branch of: severity
thrift: sympathy
thyme: courage; strength; activity
tree of life: old age
trefoil: revenge
trillium: modest beauty
truffle: surprise
tuberose: dangerous pleasures
tulip: fame
tulip, red: declaration of love
tulip, variegated: "You have beautiful eyes."
tulip, yellow: "I am hopelessly in love with you."
turnip: charity
valerian: an accommodating disposition
valerian, blue-flowered Greek: rupture
Venice sumac: intellectual excellence; splendor
Venus's-flytrap: deceit
Venus's-looking-glass: flattery
verbena: enchantment
verbena, pink: family union
verbena, scarlet: unite against evil; sensibility

verbena, white: guilelessness; "Pray for me."

veronica: fidelity

viburnum: thoughts of heaven

vine: intoxication

violet, blue: faithfulness; love; sweetness; loyalty

violet, dame: watchfulness

violet, sweet: modesty

violet, yellow: rural happiness

Virginian spiderwort: momentary happiness

virgin's bower: filial love

wake-robin: ardor

wallflower: fidelity in adversity

walnut: intellect; stratagem

water lily: purity of heart

watermelon: bulkiness

wax plant: susceptibility

wheat stalk: riches

white clover: good luck

white lily: purity; modesty

white mullein: good nature

white oak: independence

white pink: talent

white poplar: time

white rose, dried: "Death is preferable to loss of innocence."

whortleberry: treason

willow, creeping: love forsaken

willow, French: bravery and humanity

willow, water: freedom

willow, weeping: mourning

winter cherry (Chinese lantern plant): deception

wisteria: "Welcome, fair stranger"; "I cling to you."

witch hazel: a spell

wolfsbane: misanthropy

wood sorrel: joy; maternal tenderness

woodbine: fraternal love

wormwood: absence

xeranthemum: cheerfulness under adversity

yarrow: health; war

yew: sorrow

zinnia: thoughts of absent friends

XYZ

Themes and Plants

Throughout history, human beings have attached special meanings to plants. Below is a list of themes, with a corresponding list of plants, culled from many cultures around the world, including the Victorian language of flowers. Use these thematic meanings to add additional significance to the personal significance that plants already hold for you.

THEME	PLANT
absence	wormwood
abundance	wheat
accommodation	heliotrope, valerian
activity	thyme
admiration	browallia
adoration	dwarf sunflower, safflower
advice	rhubarb
affection	cinquefoil, clematis, gillyflower, honeysuckle, jonquil, locust tree, morning glory, pear blossom, periwinkle, potentilla, red dianthus, saxifrage, sorrel
affluence	peony
afterlife	bay, daffodil, laurel, lily, myrrh
age	black mulberry, chrysanthemum, Guelder rose, myrtle, tree of life
agreement	phlox, straw
ambition	hollyhock, mountain laurel
amiability	bundle of reeds, jasmine

amusement	bladder nut tree
anticipation	gooseberry
ardor	arum, wake-robin
arts	acanthus
aspiration	mountain pink
assiduousness	ivy
audacity	larch
banter	southernwood
bashfulness	peony
beauty	amaryllis, apple tree, calla lily, citron, clematis, cowslip, French honeysuckle, gladiolus, hibiscus, jasmine, laburnum, lady slipper, lily, linden, magnolia, night-blooming cereus, orchid, parti-colored daisy, rose, stock, trillium, tulip, Venetian mallow, zinnia
beneficence	marsh mallow
benevolence	potato
betrothal	carnation
birth	birch, dittany of Crete, lotus, mistletoe, silver fir
bluntness	borage
boldness	larch, pink
bonds	convolvulus
bravery	French willow, oak leaves, thyme
bride	ivy geranium, jasmine, orange flower
brotherly love	azalea, gladiolus
calmness	buckbean
celibacy	bachelor's-button
change	fir, oak, pimpernel
character	gladiolus

charity	crocus, jonquil, turnip, wild grape
charm	gardenia, orchid, ranunculus, rose, zinnia
chasteness	acadia, lily, orange blossom, violet
cheerfulness	American starwort, Chinese chrysanthemum, coreopsis, crocus, jonquil, xeranthemum
chivalry	monkshood, yellow daffodil
Christmas joy	poinsettia
clarity	fennel
cleanliness	hyssop
comfort	lavender, milkvetch, pear tree, petunia, scarlet geranium
companionship	pond lily
compassion	allspice
confidence	hepatica, lilac polyanthus, liverwort
congeniality	geranium
consecration	frankincense
consolation	red poppy, snowdrop
constancy	bellflower, bluebell, canterbury bell, cedar, hyacinth, marigold, southernwood, tulip, violet
contemplation	chrysanthemum
contentment	camellia, chrysanthemum, houstonia
cordiality	peppermint
courage	aspen, pine, poplar, thyme
creation	lotus
cure	Balm of Gilead, cranberry, swallowwort
curiosity	sycamore
death	anemone, bay, black mulberry, cypress, elder, laurel, mistletoe, myrrh, parsley, poppy, weeping willow, yew
defender	iris

delicacy	centaury, cornflower, sensitive plant, sweet pea
desire	rose
devotion	azalea, cornflower, daffodil, heliotrope, lavender, rosemary, safflower
dignity	cloves, dahlia, dianthus, elm, hundred-leaved rose, ivy, magnolia, palm, pink
distinction	cardinal flower
divinity	cowslip, lily, lotus
docility	bulrush, rush
domesticity	flax, houseleek, sage
dreams	osmunda
durability	cornel tree, dogwood, oak
eagerness	pelargonium
early death	anemone
education	cherry blossom
elation	hazelnut
elegance	acacia (pink or white), dahlia, locust tree, pomegranate flower, yellow jasmine
eloquence	crape myrtle, lotus, water lily
enchantment	mandrake, verbena
encouragement	goldenrod
endurance	aspen, carnation, oak, pine, poplar
energy	chamomile, red salvia
ephemeral glory	hibiscus
esteem	red salvia, sage, spiderwort, strawberry tree
eternal life	chrysanthemum, evergreens, holly, seaweed
eternal love	evergreens, globe amaranth
eternity	apple tree, olive tree

everlasting love	evergreens
excellence	red camellia, strawberry
faith	passion flower, pine
faithfulness	hearts' ease, heliotrope, maple, violet, wild pansy
fame	apple blossom, tulip
family	geranium, ivy, pink verbena
farewell	Michaelmas daisy
fascination	fern, honesty
fate	flax, hemp
fecundity	hollyhock
feeling	peppermint
felicity	cornflower, jasmine, sweet sultan
femininity	linden
fertility	acorn, furze, gorse, gourd, hollyhock, mandrake, mistletoe, peony, wheat
festivity	parsley
fidelity	carnation, forget-me-not, ivy, lemon blossom, lilac, plum tree, rose, rosemary, speedwell, veronica, wallflower
finesse	sweet william
flexibility	bamboo, reed
foresight	holly, strawberry blossom
forgiveness	nemophila
frankness	osier
freedom	water willow
freshness	damask rose
friendship	acacia, arborvitae, blue periwinkle, forget-me-not, geranium, ivy, jasmine, plum
frivolity	bladder nut tree, London pride

frugality	chicory, endive
fruitfulness	grape, hollyhock
funeral	walnut tree
gaiety	brussel sprouts, butterfly orchis, primrose, yellow lily
gallantry	sweet william
generosity	gladiolus, heather, orange tree
genius	plane tree, sycamore
gentility	corn cockle
gentle-heartedness	raspberry
gentleness	lamb's-ears, magnolia, wisteria
girlhood	white rosebud
gladness	myrrh
glamour	dogwood
glory	bay, daphne, laurel
good fortune	artemis leaf, daffodil, garlic, heather, ivy, mint, myrtle, narcissus, oak, peach blossom, peony, sagebrush, verbena, wheat, white clover
good will	holly, poinsettia
good wishes	basil
good-naturedness	white mullein
goodness	mercury
grace	bamboo, birch, cowslip, jasmine, rose
grandeur	ash tree
gratitude	agrimony, campanula, canterbury bell, marigold
grief	aloe, harebell, marigold, weeping birch, weeping willow
guilelessness	white verbena
happiness	Cape jasmine, gardenia, johnny-jump-up, lily-of-the-valley, marjoram, mugwort, myrtle, rosemary, Virginian spiderwort,

	yellow violet
hardiness	clematis, pine, plum
health, healing	artemisia, cornflower, Iceland moss, ivy, mistletoe, myrrh, sage, yarrow
heavenly bliss	lily
heroism	oak
home	myrtle
honesty	honesty
honor	ivy, palm
hope	almond blossom, calla lily, forget-me-not, hawthorne, jasmine, petunia, plum, snowdrop, spruce
hospitality	oak tree
humility	bindweed, broom, convolvulus, hyssop, lilac, lily-of-the-valley, morning glory, orchid, sweet woodruff, violet
imagination	lupine
immortality	acorn, balm, bay, calla lily, daphne, globe amaranth, ivy, lily, myrtle, peach, pine, sage
impatience	balsam, impatiens
incorruptibility	cedar of Lebanon
independence	white oak, wild plum tree
industry	bee orchis, flax, houseleek, red clover
ingenuity	geranium, pelargonium, white pink
innocence	alyssum, columbine, daisy, hyssop, lily, violet, white lilac
inspiration	angelica
intellect	Venice sumac, walnut
jest	southernwood
joy	burnet, Cape jasmine, crocus, gardenia, heart's ease, linden, marjoram, mugwort, oregano, parsley, wood sorrel

justice	coltsfoot, rudbeckia
kindness	raspberry
lamentation	aspen tree
levity	larkspur
liberty	live oak
life	acorn, ginseng
lightheartedness	shamrock
longevity	bamboo, chrysanthemum, fig, laurel, marigold, marjoram, mushroom, myrtle, oak tree, olive tree, orange blossom, peach blossom, plum, sage, sequoia
love	anemone, aspen, azalea, basil, basswood, betel nut, carnation, coreopsis Arkansa, daffodil, forget-me-not, furze, globe amaranth, gorse, heliotrope, honeysuckle, hyacinth, ivy, jasmine, lemon verbena, lime tree, linden, lotus flower, marjoram, moss, motherwort, myrtle, narcissus, peony, primrose, purple lilac, red catchfly, red chrysanthemum, rose, tulip, virgin's bower, woodbine, yellow acacia, yellow iris
loveliness	camellia, Indian pink, jasmine, lily, magnolia, orange blossom, rose, white hyacinth
loving thoughts	pansy
loyalty	violet
luster	crowfoot
luxury	chestnut tree
magnificence	magnolia
majesty	imperial lily, oak
marriage	betel nut, carnation, ivy, linden, myrtle, peony, rosemary
masculinity	peony
meditation	pansy

meekness	birch
melancholy	cypress
memory (-ies)	lavender, mock orange, syringa, white periwinkle
merit	cilantro, coriander, moss rose, red primrose
mildness	mallow
mirth	burnet, jonquil, larkspur, saffron crocus
modesty	hearts' ease, orchid, violet, white lily, wild pansy
mortality	pine
motherhood	cinquefoil, gourd, moss, wood sorrel
mourning	cypress, poppy, weeping birch, weeping willow, yew
music	bundle of reeds, oats
mystery	crimson polyanthus
neatness	broom
nobility	amaryllis, yellow crocus
optimism	chrysanthemum
passion	myrtle, white dittany of Crete
patience	chamomile, dock, fir tree, ox eye
patriotism	American elm, nasturtium
peace	lavender, lily, mistletoe, myrrh, myrtle, olive tree, verbana
peace of mind	hyacinth
perfection	orchid, pineapple, white lily
perseverance	canary grass, heather, laurel, southernwood, swamp magnolia, sycamore
persistence	canary grass, heather, laurel, southernwood, swamp magnolia, sycamore
philosophy	pitch pine
piety	wild geranium
play	hyacinth

pleasantness	white periwinkle
pleasure	grape, sweet pea
poetry	European sweetbrier
power	cress
preference	apple blossom, scented geranium
pride	amaryllis, gloxinia, hundred-leaved rose, polyanthus
prosperity	beech tree, evergreens, mandrake, mistletoe, peony
protection	agrimony, basil, cactus, cedar, evergreens, frankincense, garlic, holly, iris, ivy, juniper, mistletoe, mugwort, oak, rosemary, thistle
providence	purple clover
prudence	hyacinth, mountain ash
purification	frankincense, hyssop, myrrh
purity	lavender, lily-of-the-valley, lotus, orange blossom, orchid, primrose, red rosebud, Star of Bethlehem, water lily, white lily
quick-sightedness	hawkweed
radiance	ranunculus
reason	goat's rue
rebirth	calla lily, elder tree, fennel, holly, ivy, lily-of-the-valley, lotus, mistletoe, plum, pomegranate, sunflower, water lily, wheat, yew
recollection	periwinkle
reconciliation	filbert, hazel
refinement	dogwood, gardenia
regard	daffodil
regeneration	calla lily, elder tree, fennel, holly, ivy, lily-of-the-valley, lotus, mistletoe, plum, pomegranate, sunflower, water lily, wheat, yew

relief	Christmas rose, Balm of Gilead
religiousness	passion flower
remembrance	American cudweed, everlasting, marigold, pansy, rosemary, strawflower, sunflower
repentance	rue
repose	blue convolvulus, buckbean
reserve	maple
resilience	bamboo, juniper, yew
rest	mistletoe, poppy
restfulness	myrtle
revery	flowering fern
riches	wheat stalk
rigor	lantana
sacrifice	oak
sadness	cypress, dead leaves
safety	traveller's joy
sculpture	hoya
sensibility	scarlet verbena
sensitivity	mimosa, sensitive plant
sensuality	Spanish jasmine
sentiment	spearmint
silence	belladona, nightshade, Oriental poppy
simplicity	American sweetbrier, lily, mouse-ear chickweed, single rose, wild rose
sincerity	chervil
sleep	white poppy
solace	evergreen thorn
solitude	heath, lichen

sorrow	lupine, purple hyacinth, weeping birch, weeping willow, yew
splendor	Venice sumac
sport	hyacinth
stability	beech, cress, ivy, moccasin, peony
stateliness	pecan
stoicism	boxwood
strength	bamboo, blackthorn tree, cedar, fennel, oak, pine, thyme
sturdiness	oak
success	coronilla, crown vetch, plum
succor	juniper
surprise	betony
sustenance	wheat
sweetness	honeysuckle, white lily
sympathy	balm, thrift
talent	white pink
taste	scarlet fuchsia
tears	helenium
temperance	azalea, lettuce
tenderness	wood sorrel
thankfulness	agrimony
thoughts	blue salvia, hearts' ease, johnny-jump-up, orchid, pansy, violet, zinnia
thriftiness	thyme
time	fir, white poplar
tranquility	broccoli, mudwort, stonecrop
transformation	frankincense
transience	morning glory, night-blooming cereus, withered white rose
triumph	bay, laurel, oak

truth	nightshade, white chrysanthemum
unanimity	phlox
understanding	oak
union	whole straw
unity	red and white roses together
utility	grass
versatility	spruce
victory	bay, ivy, laurel, palm, parsley, purple columbine
virginity	rue
virility	ginseng
virtue	magnolia, mint, oak, rose, rue, sage
vision	rue
vitality	sycamore
vivacity	houseleek
voluptuousness	cyclamen
voraciousness	lupine
warmth	cactus, peppermint, spearmint
wedding	ivy, ivy geranium, myrtle, orange flower
welcome	wisteria
wisdom	hazel nut, sage, sequoia, white mulberry tree
wit	cuckooflower, lychnis, ragged robin
worthiness	alyssum, cilantro, coriander, fennel, pink convolvulus
youth	apple tree, daisy, grape, magnolia, plum tree, primrose, sweet pea, white mulberry
zeal, zealousness	arum, elder
zest	lemon

When my sister and I picked Kitty out of a litter at a local shelter, we could not possibly have known what an important part of our lives he would become.

Kitty was always there to comfort us whenever problems arose. He knew when somebody needed comfort and when it was a good time to play. As my sister and I grew older, we came to appreciate Kitty more and more. Kitty essentially became the glue that held our family together.

As Kitty grew older, it became harder for him to climb in through the kitty door my father had installed in a window. He had built Kitty an enclosed ramp to walk up to the window with little notches on the floor so he didn't slip. It was like a hallway leading up to the window so he wouldn't get wet in the rain or slip in the snow.

The last few years of Kitty's life, he preferred to hang around on the front porch watching people come and go. One day, along came a young female *cat that looked almost identical to Kitty. For some reason, he accepted her; she was the only cat he ever let in the yard. They became good friends and would play together. We decided after Kitty died that the female kitty had been sent there to keep my father company while he recovered from the loss of Kitty.*

Kitty died shortly after his twentieth birthday. We all felt the loss of our family member... but we talk about him now and smile.

My father felt that the least he could do was to plant a garden of memory for our Kitty since he had given so much to our family. Now, when we look out at his heart-shaped garden memorial, with his engraved stone surrounded by flowers, we know that he will always be in our heart.

—Aleta Hogan, Newfane, Vermont

We have had three wonderful dogs. Lucky loved pushing around in the woods. He's buried under a dogwood tree at the edge of the woods, and after ten years we still stop to say hello. Reggie followed us around and kept us company wherever we were working. Reggie died this winter and now lies beside his favorite pond under his dogwood tree. Winchester does his best to keep the bunnies and squirrels from eating too much of the vegetable and rose gardens. When Winchester goes, he too will be buried beside his favorite tree— a big fir tree where the squirrels climb around and yell at us if we forget to fill the feeders.

—Pam Horner, Langley, Washington

GARDEN DESIGNS

A memory garden is special because it is personal. Using the language and symbolism of plants, you can make a personal, expressive statement to or about your pet. Choosing a theme for your garden can help you clarify what it is you want to express and bring order to the design of your garden.

A garden theme develops and builds around a central idea. Many people never finish their memory garden, letting it lead them in directions they never expected. Initially, though, it can be helpful to have a plan. In the following pages are some possible starting points—places to begin to focus and define your intentions.

You know your pet better than anyone else. Let your imagination go. Find the design and plants that best celebrate your memories.

*For every
flower
that opens
in your
garden,
another
wound
is healed
in your
heart.*

Unknown

A Garden of Memory for a Cat

The message of a garden can be symbolized by the pattern it is laid out in—for example, a heart. Consider adding a birdbath to your cat's memory garden as a reminder of one of your pet's joys: birds. A statue of a cat or kitten and an engraved garden stone would also be effective complements to the garden.

Some plants to consider for a garden in memory of a cat:

Pussy willow. This small tree can be the backbone of the garden. The hallmark pearly catkins appear every spring.

Catmint. A lovely soft, gray-green mounding plant that grows to two feet high with beautiful, lavender-blue flowers from early spring to late summer. **Catnip** is a type of catmint.

Pussytoes. Pussytoes grows in a low, spreading mat of gray-green wooly foliage that has sweet, furry puffs of white-pink flowers, resembling the pads of a cat's paw, in early summer.

Pink yarrow. Yarrow is a cure for heartache in the language of flowers. This delightfully easy-to-grow plant produces pink flowers from summer through fall.

Pink dianthus. The dianthus symbolizes love and affection. This sweet plant forms a low mound of lovely blue-green foliage; the delightful pink flowers appear in late spring through summer.

Forget-me-not. This spreading plant grows up to a foot high, with tiny, profuse, exquisite blue flowers in the spring.

A Garden of Memory for a Dog

Plants such as **dianthus** and **forget-me-not** work just as well in a garden in memory of a dog as they do in a garden for a cat. And, as suggested on the previous page, you may want to consider laying the garden out in a symbolic shape.

An obvious choice for the centerpiece of a memorial for a dog is a **dogwood tree**. Other plants you might want to consider include:

Blue violet. Violets represent love, faithfulness, sweetness, and loyalty. The rich blue flowers complement the deep green foliage on this charming low-grower.

White (Shasta) daisy. A vigorous, full plant that reaches about eighteen inches in height with an abundance of beautiful blooms, the white daisy suggests innocence and simplicity.

Canterbury bell. Canterbury bell—also known as campanula, harebell, or bellflower—is the flower of gratitude. The much-loved flowers of the canterbury bell appear in June and July.

A Meditation Garden

A meditation garden can be a place to sit and remember your pet.
There are many appropriate plants to choose from.

Bee balm means *compassion* and *consolation*.
Canterbury bell is the flower of *gratitude*.
Daisy connotes *innocence* and *simplicity*.
Lamb's ear speaks of *healing*.
Lemon-scented geranium symbolizes *tranquility*.
Locust tree is the symbol of *natural change*
and *"affection beyond the grave."*

Viburnum (snowball) represents *thoughts of heaven*.
White rose means *love* and *silence*.

The colors of these plants are significant. Purple is the color of spirit; blue is the color of peace; and white is the color of purity and silence. The green foliage reflects healing.

A meditation garden might be designed symmetrically to symbolize the importance of the balance a spiritual life moves toward. It has the feeling of solitude as the plants wrap around and enclose the sitting area. A statue of a religious figure of your choosing might sit in the center diamond as a focal point. An unobtrusive pebble path can lend tranquility.

A Bird and Butterfly Garden

The best landscaping plan to attract birds and butterflies includes a variety of native plants. Evergreen trees such as the **spruce** provide escape cover for birds, winter shelter, and summer nesting sites; they also provide seeds from the pinecones. Birds will visit the spent flower heads of **echinacea (purple coneflower)** and **sunflowers**, grasping on to the swaying plant as they peck out the seeds. Tubular flowers, such as **bee balm**, are especially attractive to hummingbirds. Birds can be further encouraged to visit your garden with bird feeders, houses, and baths.

Butterflies like to light on the flat flower heads of plants such as **yarrow**, **coreopsis**, and **daisies**. Or, if you prefer, you can purchase butterfly houses at many garden centers. Much like birds, butterflies need protection from the wind, a place to lay their eggs, and water to drink. To attract monarch butterflies, plant **milkweed** in your garden.

Other bird and butterfly attracters include:

Aster	**Lavender**
Buddleia (butterfly bush)	**Lupine**
Butterfly weed	**Morning glory**
Cosmos	**Parsley**
Cotoneaster	**Petunia**
Crab apple	**Phlox**
Currant shrub	**Pincushion flower**
Delphinium	**Rosemary**
Dill	**Russian sage**
Fennel	**Shrubby cinquefoil**
Globe amaranth	**Thyme**
Honeysuckle	**Viburnum**
	Zinnia

A Spring Garden of Memory

As nature comes alive in the spring, a garden bursting forth with foliage and flowers can symbolize the cycle of life and your undying love for your pet. A spring bulb garden is relatively easy to plant and maintain, but it needs to be prepared in the fall. Below are some flowering bulbs and perennials with special significance.

Lily-of-the-valley symbolizes a *return of happiness.*
Purple hyacinth speaks of *sorrow.*
Red tulip is a *declaration of love.*
Snowdrop is the emblem of *hope and consolation.*

Sprinkle seeds of **forget-me-nots** over the newly planted soil for additional meaning and a longer bloom period.

An Herb Garden of Memory

Well known for their healing properties, herbs are steeped in meaning and history. With rich scents, a variety of textures, and multiple uses, an herb garden evokes a deep engagement with nature through the senses. Here are several herbs to consider.

Germander is the herb of *joy*.
Mint speaks of *grief*.
Oregano speaks of *joy* and *happiness*.
Peppermint symbolizes *wisdom*.
Rosemary is the herb of *remembrance*.
Rue symbolizes *grief* and *understanding*.
Silver thyme symbolizes *remembering our happiness*.
Tansy means *life everlasting*.
Thyme reflects *courage*.

All my animal friends have a place in my garden. I have covered their graves with violets, hostas, lilies, and daffodils. My memorial to them is a natural setting: flowers, trees, and shrubs. I also memorialize them by going to the pound and giving a home to an unwanted dog or cat. Even though these animals may only be with me for a short time, they will be loved and cared for. As I write this, at my feet lies Corky, a little five-year-old Corgi that was sent with her new puppies to the pound because she inconveniently got pregnant. She looks like a little red fox and is so loving and obedient. She and I will enjoy each other's company for as long as we shall have together.

—Shirley Norman, Markleysburg, Pennsylvania

5

PREPARING, INSTALLING, AND MAINTAINING YOUR GARDEN

*W*hile memorial gardens are special, created out of love, they still require labor to prepare, install, and maintain. Fortunately, the physical effort it takes to make a garden can often be a useful expenditure of energy. Sleep, for instance, is often negatively affected by grief. Sometimes when grieving, you need the physical release that a challenging project will take.

You may find comfort in inviting friends or family to help with the installation. Find people who are willing to listen and honor your feelings. Ask them to help you build your memorial garden so you can talk and reminisce as you commune with the healing forces of nature.

Life begins the day you start a garden.

Chinese proverb

Preparation

STEP 1

Mark out the edges of your border. Typically irregular, curved edges blend best with landscapes. Use a garden hose to lay out the edges and curves to help you visualize the dimensions and shape of the garden.

STEP 2

Remove the sod, as well as all roots of anything currently growing in the space. (Watering well a day or two before will make this job easier.)

STEP 3

Till the soil to a depth of at least eight inches. Break up clods of soil and remove any rocks. Optional: If you have the time, at this point you may water, wait two weeks, and then remove any new growth. Turn over the soil again. This can eliminate a good portion of problematic weeds and grass in your garden.

STEP 4

Add generous quantities of the best compost you can find. All soil types benefit from adding quality compost. A four-inch layer is sufficient for average soils. If your soil is particularly poor, add several more inches.

STEP 5

Following the directions on the package, add a slow-release, complete organic fertilizer. Be sure that the fertilizer you use meets local guidelines. Phosphorous is banned is some areas because it encourages algae bloom in lakes and rivers.

STEP 6

Thoroughly mix the compost and fertilizer into the existing soil. Rake smooth.

Installation

STEP 7

Most nursery plants and seedlings can be planted in early spring, usually as soon as the soil can be worked in your area. Do not allow purchased plants to become overly dry before you plant them. Choose an overcast or cool day to plant. If this is not possible, plant in the early evening. Generally you should plant with the top of the potted soil even with the garden soil surface. If the plant roots are matted, slice the bound roots with a knife in several places or tease apart the root ball's surface.

If you are planting from seed, follow the directions on the seed packet. Some seeds should be planted in the fall; others can be started indoors in late winter or early spring, or planted directly into the ground in the spring when the ground temperature is sufficiently warm.

Note: Typically, plants have been hardened-off (acclimated to outdoor weather) by the nursery. If not, or if you are starting the plants indoors from seeds, you must take a few days to harden them. Begin by bringing them outside for several hours, gradually increasing the time until they are acclimated to outdoor conditions.

STEP 8

Water thoroughly. This is essential, even if the soil is moist. This step ensures that the roots are in contact with the soil.

Step 9

Mulch, preferably with ground bark or bark chips. Mulching retains moisture, reduces weed growth, and greatly enhances your final project's appearance.

Maintenance

Your garden will need more water as the plants establish their root systems and adjust to their new home, particularly during the first season. Keep the soil moist, not wet, in the beginning, gradually decreasing your watering schedule. The following season, water as indicated for your climate, always watering deeply to encourage deep root growth, which makes for hardier plants.

Removing spent blooms (deadheading) prevents seed formation. The plants use that energy for increased vigor and often another round of blooms.

Plant disease is best approached by prevention. Healthy plants are much less susceptible to pests or disease. Purchase only plants with healthy foliage. Maintain an appropriate watering schedule. Keep weeds at bay. Make sure your plants have nutrients by fertilizing them regularly. Do what you can to attract birds to your yard to dine on garden pests. If these measures are not sufficient, natural, organic products that address plant infestations are available at your local nursery.

After the growing season and your plants have gone dormant, remove the dead foliage to reduce disease carryover to the next season. Also, mulch the bed with leaves, wood chips, peat moss, or other types of organic mulch to retain moisture and reduce plant damage from temperature fluctuations.

Before each subsequent growing season, top-dress your garden's soil with two to three inches of quality compost or add an organic fertilizer to ensure your plants have the nutrients they need for another season.

Each state has extension offices that offer a wealth of information about local horticulture concerns. They can answer questions about your region's typical soil, plant diseases, the local gardening zone, the first and last frost dates for your area, and many other topics.

Laddie and Inky

I have always greatly mourned the deaths of my pets, but I was absolutely devastated when my tuxedo cats, Laddie and Inky, died. Their deaths showed me that no matter how hard you try to protect your loved ones, sometimes you don't have a say in the matter. I was surprised at the depth of my grief and wondered if others felt the same way I did when their pets died. I talked with several people who had also lost beloved pets and found they had had similar experiences.

I decided to prepare a lasting memorial, not only to Inky and Laddie, but to my other pets as well. The cats had always loved to play in the woods, so this seemed a fitting place for a memory garden. I had started a pet cemetery there about fifteen years earlier. Now I set about cleaning it up and making it beautiful. On the corner of the garden is a big tree giving it shade. In the garden I have planted spring lilies and mums to symbolize the renewal of life. The flowers in the garden are the colors of the rainbow—a sign of hope.

All the pets have their own stepping-stone above their gravesite. I have added figurines and an angel to the garden, and am in the process of painting the names of each of my pets on a retaining wall block to be placed over their stepping-stone. To finish my cemetery I hung solar lights on a pole to symbolize the light guiding the way for my pets that have crossed over. All my pets have given me wonderful years of enjoyment and love, and this is the way that I memorialize their presence in my life.

—Diane Newman, Ozark, Missouri

6

FINISHING TOUCHES

*A*ccessories such as benches, chairs, arbors, trellises, statuary, birdhouses, birdbaths, bird feeders, paths, walkways, plaques, engraved stones, and artificial lighting can provide a finishing touch to your memory garden project. Carefully chosen accessories can turn an ordinary garden into a truly special one. Whether the purpose is functional or purely ornamental, accessories can enhance the inspirational quality of your memory garden. Use your personal taste and preferences to add depth and texture to your garden.

A garden is a friend you can visit anytime.

Unknown

Garden Furniture

A place to sit is essential in a garden of tribute. You need a place where you can linger and let your concerns melt away. What better way to connect with the spirit and memory of your pet and touch the warmth within your own heart than by sitting in a beautiful spot of nature created in love? Whether you take a cup of tea, a book, or just your thoughts with you to the garden, you will want a place to rest comfortably.

Garden furniture need not be grand, ornate, or expensive. Different regions of the country feature different materials and bench styles. In the Rocky Mountains, sandstone is popular. New England gardens commonly have Adirondack-style benches and chairs. Battery-style park benches are easy to find and affordable. Rustic styling has become more popular over the years, and garden centers are beginning to carry more of this unique outdoor furniture. Classic lines in traditional teak or cedar are handsome in any landscape and are weather-resistant. The Monet garden bench has an arched ladder-back design. Weatherized wicker is comfortable and inviting. Cast iron furniture is durable and easy to maintain.

Wooden furniture needs to be maintained with regular applications of a quality wood sealer. Even naturally weather-resistant woods such as teak, cedar, or redwood benefit from periodic sealing. Depending on the extremes of your particular climate and the type of garden furniture you choose, you may need to protect or shelter your furniture during the winter.

Within the appropriate place, a garden swing is a great alternative to a garden bench. If it fits into your landscape, a tree swing or a freestanding unit recalls a simpler way of life. Gentle rocking provides a relaxing vantage from which to view your garden.

Many garden benches and swings can be personalized with an engraved inscription on a small brass plaque.

Arbors and Trellises

Memory gardens are refuges. An arbor at the entry to a memory garden can set a garden off from the rest of your property, creating privacy and sanctuary. Nestling within an arbor planted with **morning glories** or heavenly-scented **climbing roses** can give you moments of sweet repose for remembering the gift of your beloved pet. In addition to providing an entry gate or alcove for seating, arbors also provide shelter from the sun on hot summer days.

Arbors come in a wide variety of styles—and a wide variety of materials, including redwood, cedar, rustic twig, copper tubing, vinyl, wrought iron, and cast aluminum.

Among the many vines that can be grown on an arbor, **grapes** and **climbing roses** are long-standing favorites. In very warm climates, **bougainvillea** provides stunning color. For cooler zones, the versatile **clematis** is a good choice. **Passionflower**, which is traditionally associated with Christian faith, is a symbolically appropriate vine for a memory garden. **Honeysuckle**, with its unmistakable fragrance, pleases both the eye and the nose. Other possibilities include **silver-lace vine**, **trumpet vine**, and **Virginia creeper**, or **woodbine**.

If you don't have room for an arbor, you may want to consider a decorative trellis. Like arbors, trellises provide support for climbing vines, and, like arbors, they come in many different shapes, sizes, and materials.

Statuary

Statuary is another accessory that can enhance your garden. Whatever type of statue you choose—traditional or contemporary, sophisticated or rustic, serious or lighthearted—all that matters is that it speaks to you.

Many people will create their garden around a statue that resembles their lost pet. Others add animal statuary for its "natural" appearance. And still others use animals as symbols—for example, the elephant as a symbol of sagacity, the lion as a symbol of courage, the bluebird as a symbol of happiness, the lark as a symbol of joy, the rabbit as a symbol of resourcefulness, the swan as a symbol of purity, the fish as a symbol of good luck, the dove as a symbol of peace, the owl as a symbol of wisdom, and the turtle as a symbol of endurance. You can find animal statuary at many garden centers, and statues of specific breeds of pets can also be located by searching the Internet.

Religious figures are obvious choices for a memory garden, reinforcing, as they do, the garden's spirit and purpose. Some figures you might select include St. Francis of Assisi, the patron saint of nature; St. Fiacre, the patron saint of gardeners; Kuan Yin, the compassionate Buddha; Jesus' Mother Mary, another symbol of compassion; angels and cherubs; or Shiva, the Hindu god, destroyer of illusion. Animal figures with specifically Christian implications include the fish (Christ), the pelican (redemption), and the dove (God's promise to man and Christ's resurrection),

For a more whimsical touch, consider fantastic subjects such as garden sprites and fairies.

Birdbaths, Houses, and Feeders

A vast array of birdbaths, houses, and feeders are available if you would like to indulge in the pleasures of birdwatching. In addition to attracting birds, birdbaths, houses, and feeders can add delightful decorative elements to a garden.

The proper combination of quality materials and good design makes an effective birdhouse. If you have specific species of birds you want to attract, go to a birding center to be certain the home you purchase will invite the species you want.

Birdbaths and feeders should be placed where predators, particularly domesticated cats, and food thieves, particularly squirrels, can't get to them easily.

Seed-eating birds are the most common visitors to the backyard. Sunflower seeds are a favored food for a number of desirable species and are considered by many to be the most effective way to attract the greatest number of birds. In the wintertime, suet feeders will attract woodpeckers, nuthatches, finches, and other species. To attract hummingbirds, hang one or more feeders that dispense sweet nectar. Be sure to clean the feeders and change the liquid frequently.

For suggestions on creating a bird and butterfly garden, see pages 78–79.

Paths and Walkways

Many garden designs have a walkway leading to a sitting area. Both the walkway and the area in front of the bench need to be paved with stepping-stones, pebbles, or other material to prevent the ground from becoming muddy. Ordinary bricks can be used as well, as can any preformed paving stone from a home supply center. Garden centers can usually direct you to a stone yard that sells flagstone-type paving materials, as each area of the country has a stone indigenous to its geology. Stepping-stones can also be made from large logs sliced in pieces three to four inches thick and then treated with a wood preservative. Some artisans make stepping-stones from stained glass in an array of beautiful designs, which are then weather-treated and preserved with a sealant. For the do-it-yourselfer, forms are available to make your own cobblestone-type path from concrete, allowing you to mix the cement yourself and add a colorant of your liking. To soften the look of the path, plant grass or a low ground cover between the pavers. Low-growing varieties of **thyme** are especially suited for this type of planting.

Plaques and Engraved Stones

A garden of tribute is intensely personal, a place to express what is in your heart. Plaques and engraved stones are one more way to add rich meaning to the space. Favorite inscriptions, original poetry, birth dates, inspirational quotes, prayers, and, of course, your pet's name are all examples of things you can have engraved on a stone or plaque. Stone yards can help you find a stonecutter in your area. Every area has local artists who work with different materials. If you choose a wooden plaque, be sure to seal it with a quality wood preservative.

Whether you hang the engraving on a wall, nail it to the trunk of a tree, or nestle it in a border at the edge of the garden, adding an inscription is a wonderful way to declare the intent of your garden.

Lighting

Lighting can also be used to impact the ambiance of outdoor areas and to increase the amount of time comfortably available to you. Illuminating paths, statuary, and other garden features brings a different dimension to the garden at night. Casting a light upwards on a special tree or shrub creates a feeling of expansive peacefulness.

As with other garden accessories, there are many types and styles of lighting to choose from. Non-ornamental lights can be placed behind or beneath plants and other garden features to give a garden texture and depth. Ornamental lighting can visually complement the design and symbolism of a garden. Common styles of ornamental lighting include contemporary, Mission, and Japanese.

Lighting can be placed in a garden in numerous ways: directional flood lamps, Malibu lamps, surface-mounted step lights, post lights, column fixtures, wall-mounted lights, hanging lights, well lights, fiber optic lights, and rope lighting. Garden torches and solar-powered lights are convenient methods of illumination because they do not involve wiring the garden for electricity. However, one advantage of wiring the garden is that you can put your light system on an automatic timer. In addition to adding beauty and charm to your garden, this can also make your home safer.

Water and Other Options

Water is an important element in any garden. Not only do plants depend on it, but water can be used to attract wildlife, complement the design of your garden, diversify the plants you can use, make a garden appear more natural, and create a more soothing, tranquil atmosphere. Adding water to a garden doesn't have to be complicated. In addition to birdbaths, there are many compact and simple outdoor fountains and pre-formed ponds for you to choose from. Another option well suited for a memory garden is a wishing well, which may or may not contain water.

From the serious to the whimsical, from the antique to the modern, the array of garden accessories is vast. You can buy a sur-

prising range of sundials, wind chimes, copper or brass art, obelisks, and gazing balls. A browse through one of the many garden supply catalogs, a stroll through a good-sized garden center, or time spent on the Internet will inspire you to complete and complement your garden of memory in your own unique way.

7

DEDICATING YOUR GARDEN

Throughout history, every culture and every religion has acknowledged death with some sort of ritual or ceremony. The ritual, whether holding a funeral, sitting Shiva, or scattering ashes, orients the survivors in the midst of their grief and is an important step in the healing process.

The installation of your garden might be completed with a ceremony dedicating this space to your pet's memory. Creating the garden directs the energy of your grief toward healing. Engaging in a completion ritual is another big step along the path. With gardening complete, a dedication ritual brings your intention into sharper focus. You have invested yourself in this process of creation for a reason. This garden celebrates the life and love you shared. It honors what has past, a tangible, visible reflection of a

Cry
if you
must,
but
plant
if you
can.

Kay
Frey

Leila

My buddy Leila Pninah came to live with me in the fall of 1989. Over the years Leila became a being of great depth and sweetness. In December of 2000 we discovered a fibrosarcoma growing at the back of her neck. By the summer of 2001 it was clear that she would not survive much longer. I had spent much time working with grief, loss, and transitions both personally and professionally as an art therapist specializing in bereavement work, but I had never before been directly involved in the process of dying. It was profound.

Because she was charcoal-gray, I had named her Leila, which means "night" in Hebrew. Her naming had also followed the Jewish tradition of naming someone after a dead relative: my sister's family had previously had a cat named Leila. I added Pninah during her last phase. Pninah means "pearl" in Hebrew. I had often called her my dark pearl, Leila Pninah, as an endearment.

Leila died a "good death," a week after her twelfth birthday, at home in my arms, gently and quietly, wagging her glorious long tail as she went to sleep. Our patient veterinarian sat with us, talking with me about her life. Later several friends came by, and we buried her on the hill by my house, wrapped in a cloth I had painted with prayers and gentle wishes. I covered her grave with a large rock, both as protection against digging critters and as a spot to sit on and take in the view. It is a rock she would have enjoyed, as I do.

It took months for me to complete a memorial peace pole at the gravesite, which I had envisioned in the first week after her death. On the post I wood-burned her name, dates, and the word "levav" in Hebrew script. A dear friend who is a rabbi suggested this word, which means "of or in the heart." It appears in a verse in the book of Samuel that speaks of how people see what is visible, but God sees into the heart.

The deep love that Leila and I shared was clearly a heart connection, and I will remain ever grateful for her presence and her memory.

—Sandra Laemmle, Lyons, Colorado

life that was lived and will be remembered. The ceremony also acknowledges the spirit inherent in life, inherent in the natural world—life always changing, always moving forward, always evolving from one level of awareness to the next.

Extend much compassion toward yourself when preparing to dedicate your garden. Rituals are powerful. The dedication is a step to be taken with consciousness. The most meaningful ceremonies are individualized to reflect the life being honored and the lives touched by the loss. Therefore, the following suggestions are offered only as starting points. Spend time contemplating and discussing what you and others involved want to incorporate into this time. Reflect on the gifts you received from your companion animal. In what ways are you a better person for having had him or her in your life?

It may help to remember your life with pet in a linear fashion. What were the treasures uncovered on your journey together? Elevate your mind to the highest point of view possible. See the places in your heart touched by this being. Through the memories and the sorrow, see if you can find the sweet gratitude for what you shared and for the place your soul has now brought you. Contemplate, from the highest mind and heart, what your grief has taught you. Consciously choose what you will hold as most important from this experience. Release any remaining residue of guilt and resentment, of judgment toward yourself, your departed pet, or anyone else. Vow to come through this to a place of increased awareness of the purity and perfection of life in all its raw, stinging forms.

When you are ready, open your heart and dedicate this spot of heaven on earth in the spirit of highest truth, utmost beauty, deepest integrity, and unconditional love.

REMEMBRANCE RITUALS

- Set aside a specific time for the ritual. If you like, invite others to be present.

- Ask for spiritual support at the ceremony.

- Incorporate the natural ceremonial elements of fire and water.

- Display favorite pictures.

- Reflect on and share favorite memories.

- Share what you will miss.

- Talk about something you learned from this special animal.

- Read poems that speak meaningfully to you, or write one of your own.

- Incorporate spiritual readings that are meaningful to you.

- Write, and read, a letter to your pet.

- State your intentions for the garden. Say whatever feels right to you.

- Use this time to place an engraved stone or statue in the garden.

- Scatter your pet's ashes in the garden, if that is what you have chosen.

- In future years, share seeds or plant slips from this special garden.

Old Dog

by Stephen C. Behrendt

What am I to do with you, then?
Half blind, nearly toothless, bony paws waggling in dream-chase,
you lie there, who cannot even walk
some days, when the arthritis swells your joints.
And on those days, on those cold gray November afternoons,
those premature, mizzling March evenings,
when I carry you nearer the fire,
your eyes, your deep hazel eyes,
speak something that is not pain; your tail moves slowly.
We grow old, my friend;
you are my companion, my fore-shadow.

Is it misery to be so, to be stiff, and still to dream;
to run breathless miles now only in sleep;
to be carried, carefully, like a full cup of tea,
merely to feel the fire's warmth on your trembling flanks?
Would you be out of this, then;
would you be away, dead, gone who knows where,
but leaving my stove-side vacant, incomplete,
your pillow put into the trash, as though you had never lived,
as though our eyes had never met, before yours clouded blue,
our needs never converged these empty winter nights?
Do I love you, somehow, or you me,
or have we merely shared a time and space,
a cabin with a fire, some little food?

You have earned your warm place, your meals
softened in my kitchen, spooned when you cannot lift your head.
They are yours, and I should carry you always,
burn this house to warm you.
Do I owe you, at last, death? Is that dignity, finally?
I am your torment, then, withholding what I might give,
outside with my knife, my gun.
I shall try to make you easy in your grief
for I am selfish
both for myself now, watching you sleep,
and for myself someday, some deep day, only remembering.
Sleep, old friend: I shall not be your death
though we share a thousand winters at this fire,
I gazing at your dark side, watching you breathe,
losing you at every moment,
grieving for us both, indistinguishable,
while outside the soft snow falls in silence.

Patience

The card read, "The Saddest Day With Your Dog Was Also The Kindest." It was from our veterinarian. But I didn't feel kind as I dug our dog's grave in the backyard, in the rain. Sixteen years earlier, I had picked her from a litter of little white furballs, and from the moment I saw her I knew she was the one. For weeks I had begged my husband to let me get a small housedog. He had finally agreed, on the condition that I name the dog "Patience" as a reminder for me to be patient. It didn't take long to find out that neither of us was very patient, so I nicknamed her "Putzie." Putzie's love and devotion carried me through several major life changes—a divorce, a long-distance move, and a chronic illness, to name a few. We were more than best friends.

In her later years, a collapsed trachea caused Putzie to cough whenever she got excited. At times the coughing was so bad that she would become disoriented, stumble, and fall. When this happened, I would hold her and talk to her until she recognized me again. I didn't want to face the fact that she was *fading. I asked our vet how one knows when it's time to say goodbye. He told me*

to ask Patience by looking in her eyes. Those eyes, once so full of wonderment and

excitement for life, were now dull and tired. They were asking me to let her go.

On the evening we took her in, my husband and I sat in the car saying

goodbye to our friend, my little girl. Tears trickled down our faces as the rain

did on the car. The process was bittersweet and final. The moment Patience

died we felt her spirit leave her body.

We buried Putzie's body in the backyard by flashlight in the rain. As we

turned to walk away, the
clouds above us parted to
reveal a grand display of stars.
Days later I painted some
rocks white and placed them
around her grave. An angel
looks on for protection, and
lily-of-the-valley is planted
there as well.

—Sandra S. Nelson,
Vancouver, Washington

The Rainbow Bridge

Just this side of heaven is a place called Rainbow Bridge.

When an animal dies that has been especially close to someone here, that pet goes to Rainbow Bridge. There are meadows and hills for all of our special friends so they can run and play together. There is plenty of food, water, and sunshine, and our friends are warm and comfortable.

All the animals that had been ill and old are restored to health and vigor. Those who were hurt or maimed are made whole and strong again, just as we remember them in our dreams of days and times gone by. The animals are happy and content, except for one small thing; they each miss someone very special to them, who had to be left behind.

They all run and play together, but the day comes when one suddenly stops and looks into the distance. His bright eyes are intent. His eager body quivers. Suddenly he begins to run from the group, flying over the green grass, his legs carrying him faster and faster.

You have been spotted, and when you and your special friend finally meet, you cling together in joyous reunion, never to be parted again. The happy kisses rain upon your face; your hands again caress the beloved head, and you look once more into the trusting eyes of your pet, so long gone from your life but never absent from your heart.

Then you cross Rainbow Bridge together....

—author unknown

FINAL THOUGHTS

8

When my brother died a number of years ago, the question arose how best to memorialize him. Because he was an avid gardener and his death took place at a hospice, we chose to donate money to the hospice for a garden that would reflect the person he was. We felt this would be a gift to future residents, as well as to visitors and staff.

It wasn't until after we made this decision that I came to understand why David had spent so much time outside, digging and planting in the dirt. I discovered that when I spent time outside I felt tuned into all of creation—the expansive sky, the movement of air, the sounds of birds, the activity going on within the soil. These all pointed to a much larger picture. I began to find understanding in the cycles of the seasons—birth, death, dormancy, and renewal.

One is nearer God's Heart in a garden Than anywhere else on earth.

Dorothy Frances Gurney

I came to see that I was powerless to control the forces of nature, whether it was a strong wind blowing over tender young stalks or a deer grazing on my long-awaited blooms.

I found peace in accepting the inevitability of natural occurrences. Experiencing nature in a deeply intimate way transformed my life as the connections made outside integrated within.

Through my professional and personal experience, I have learned that unresolved grief—be it from a recent loss or one more distant—leaves a residue in our being, and each subsequent loss taps into that unresolved grief. It can result in a numbing effect, a lingering anger or sadness, but the result is the same. Our true essence becomes clouded.

My wish for you is that you know healing from the pain of loss, that you know the peace of acceptance that transcends all circumstances, and that you know, in honoring the memory of the beloved pet that graced and blessed your life, you have blessed this earth with a healing garden made with love.

A chilly autumn day in the park was warmed for me by the appearance of a skinny, bedraggled kitten. With her enchanting and radiant spirit, she immediately tugged at my heartstrings. Misty and I quickly discovered that we were soul mates. I told her that I'd always take care of her. She was my gift of pure love. Misty enjoyed many years of carefree, excellent health. But at seventeen her aging body began to show signs of weakening and then sickness. Finally, the time came for her to leave her exhausted body.

Filled with anguish, I carried Misty outside to my small garden. I wanted her to feel the warmth of summer on her fur, smell the fresh air, and see the greenery around her for one last time. Enveloped by the comforting presence and love of family and friends, and with the help of our veterinarian, my beloved cat expired peacefully in my arms. As she drew her last breath, the sun suddenly filtered through the trees, beaming brightly upon her, as if the angels were there to bring her to the light.

I have never felt such intense grief, or so empty and consumed with sadness. A friend suggested that I create a memorial garden. The process of planning the garden brought immense healing to me. It was comforting just to browse through seed, plant, and garden statuary catalogs for ideas. Shopping for Misty's garden brought such joy. Though no artist, I painted the tribute sign for the garden myself, complete with gold paw prints and lettering. As spring approached, I hired landscapers to prepare the ground and fertilize the soil for planting. After the landscapers finished their work, I realized that the garden had been dug in the shape of a cat with wings—a cat angel!

Soon it was time to plant the garden. Prayers opened the process, and from then on I felt Misty's presence around me. I placed her tribute sign in the garden and planted catnip underneath it. I also planted bleeding heart,

gold-leaf hydrangea, lilies, roses, sage, mint, St. John's wort, penstemon, lavender, and other plants of special significance. The remaining space was filled with colorful flowers interspersed with decorative stepping-stones, small rocks from sacred places, charming garden flags, and statues of cats, angels, fairies, and St. Francis.

Every year the garden grows more beautiful. Gazing out on it always brings joy and contentment to my soul. On the 25th of every month I go to Misty's garden and settle myself at the spot where Misty exhaled her last breath. There I pray that the time will come when all animals are loved, valued, and respected for the beauty and love that each of them radiates. I believe that day will bring a holy oneness and peace to all beings on the planet.

—Judith A. Ruta, Liverpool, New York

SELECTED PLANTS
ARRANGED BY COMMON NAME

The following plants have been selected for their special significance for memorializing a pet. This list is in no way intended to be comprehensive. It is merely offered as a starting point as you consider what sort of living tribute is most appropriate for your particular situation.

There are countless species, varieties, and cultivars of plants for you to choose from. To locate those that are best suited for the region in which you live, visit local garden centers and nurseries. Some plants have a soil pH preference—which is to say that they prefer soil that is either alkaline or acid. To determine the type of soil you have in your garden, contact your local county extension office. For specific planting and gardening information, there are many excellent gardening publications and resources available.

Common Name	*Botanical Name*	Type	Zone	Light
acacia	*Acacia*	evergreen shrub or tree	7-10	full sun
aloe	*Aloe*	succulent	9-10	full sun to partial shade
anemone (windflower)	*Anemone*	flowering bulb or perennial	6-10	full sun to partial shade
artemisia (tarragon)	*Artemisia*	perennial shrub or herb	3-10	full sun
aster, hardy (Michaelmas daisy)	*Aster*	perennial	4-9	full sun
baby's breath	*Gypsophila*	perennial or annual	3-9	full sun

Comments

The acacia symbolized birth and death for the ancient Egyptians. In Europe, it symbolizes immortality. There are many types, all of which produce tiny yellow flowers.

Aloe symbolized grief in the Victorian language of flowers. It can be grown as a houseplant in northern zones if taken outdoors in the summer and kept in a well-lighted, dry place in the winter. Produces flowers in the spring.

The name "anemone" is derived from the Greek word for wind, and the flower is also known as the "windflower." The anemone evokes the transitoriness of life and traditionally symbolizes an early death. It is associated with the death of Adonis in ancient Greek mythology and with the blood of saints in Christianity. In Chinese folklore, anemones are planted over graves. Colors include white, mauve, lavender, pink, crimson, blue, rose, and scarlet.

In classical mythology, artemisia was sacred to Artemis (Diana) and believed to have healing qualities. Artemisia is valued for its aromatic gray-green or silver foliage. Also known as tarragon, wormwood, southernwood, or dusty miller.

Asters are a large and diverse group of plants with masses of daisy-like flowers. Most varieties bloom from late summer into fall. Flowers are white, blue, red, pink, or lavender with yellow centers. Good for cut flowers. Also called Michaelmas daisy.

Baby's breath is a summer bloomer, producing tiny, airy white or pink blossoms in large clusters. An excellent cut or dried flower.

Common Name	Botanical Name	Type	Zone	Light
balm (lemon balm)	*Melissa officinalis*	annual herb	all	full sun or partial shade
bamboo	several genera	evergreen shrub	7-10	full sun
basil, sweet or ornamental	*Ocimum basilicum*	annual herb	all	full sun
bee balm (bergamot)	*Monarda didyma*	perennial	4-9	full sun to partial shade
birch	*Betula*	deciduous tree	2-4	full sun
bougainvillea	*Bougainvillea*	evergreen vine	9-10	full sun to partial shade
brunnera	*Brunnera*	perennial	4-5	partial shade

Comments

Balm, or lemon balm, is a traditional symbol for immortality. It signifies sympathy in the Victorian language of flowers and was often used in memorials. Produces small white or yellow flowers in late summer and early fall that are very attractive to bees.

In China, bamboo symbolizes resiliency in the face of adversity. These members of the grass family have slender, arching stems and feathery foliage. Most grow rapidly.

Because basil is the most sacred of all plants to Hindus, it is planted on Hindu graves, and each believer is buried with a basil leaf. Its aromatic leaves repel mosquitoes. Tiny white or purplish flowers appear in late summer.

Bee balm, or bergamot, grows in bushy clumps, 2 to 4 feet tall, 2 to 3 feet wide. Clusters of pink, red, or lavender flowers are much loved by hummingbirds and bees.

In Celtic folklore, the birch represented the birth of new life. The weeping birch, like the weeping willow, is a symbol of grief. Foliage turns yellow in the fall.

A drought-resistant, twining vine, suitable only for the warmest zones or greenhouses. Produces beautiful clusters of purple, white, orange, or red flowers.

Brunnera produces blue star-like flowers in mid to late spring. The early appearance of blooms make brunnera a good companion for spring-flowering bulbs. Also called Siberian forget-me-not and Siberian bugloss.

Common Name	Botanical Name	Type	Zone	Light
butterfly bush (buddleia)	*Buddleia*	deciduous shrub	5-10	full sun
butterfly weed	*Asclepias*	perennial	4-10	full sun
calendula (pot marigold)	*Calendula officinalis*	annual	all	full sun
campanula (bellflower)	*Campanula*	biennial or perennial	3-10	full sun to partial shade
catmint (catnip)	*Nepeta*	perennial	3-10	full sun
cattail (bulrush)	*Typha*	perennial	4-10	full sun
centaurea (cornflower)	*Centaurea*	perennial or annual	4-10	full sun

Comments

Butterfly bush, or buddleia, is fast-growing and hardy. Varieties range from 4 to 15 feet in height. White, purple, red, pink, lilac, or blue flowers appear in early to late summer.

Butterfly weed is a common wildflower, related to the milkweed, valued for its clusters of orange flowers in summer, as well as its attractive foliage and distinctive seedpods.

Calendula, or pot marigold, grows 1 to 2 feet tall and blooms throughout the summer. Flowers are orange, yellow, or cream. A good cut flower.

Campanula, also known as bellflower, canterbury bell, or harebell, produces flowers that are blue, purple, pink, or white. Its sturdy erect stems help make it an excellent cut flower. Smaller varieties are good choices for rock gardens.

Catmint produces gray-green leaves and spikes of purple flowers in summer. Although a favorite of cats, catnip (*N. cataria*) is not particularly ornamental.

This distinctive shallow-water plant—with its flat, pointed leaves, tall, sturdy stalks, and dark brown flower spikes—is a hardy addition to a water garden. An invasive grower, it needs to be planted in a container.

The cornflower was a popular flower among the ancient Egyptians who often used it in funeral tributes for the dead. It is traditionally associated with healing. Perennial varieties are generally referred to as centaurea. Annual varieties are commonly called cornflower, bachelor's-button, dusty miller, or sweet-sultan. All make good cut flowers.

Common Name	Botanical Name	Type	Zone	Light
chrysanthemum	Chrysanthemum	perennial	4-10	full sun
cinquefoil (potentilla)	Potentilla	perennial or deciduous shrub	2-10	full sun or partial shade
clematis	Clematis	perennial vine	4-10	full sun to partial shade
coreopsis (tickseed)	Coreopsis	perennial	3-9	full sun
cosmos	Cosmos	annual	all	full sun to partial shade
cotoneaster	Cotoneaster	deciduous or evergreen shrub	2-8	full sun or partial shade

Comments

Known in parts of southern Europe as "Fiori dei Morte" (the flower of death), the chrysanthemum was traditionally offered to the dead on All Saints Day. A symbol of eternal life, it is closely associated with funerals. Flowers are white, red, pink, orange, yellow, purple, lavender, or russet.

Cinquefoil, or potentilla, is a hardy plant that requires little attention once it is established. Small yellow, white, or pink flowers appear throughout the summer. Varieties range from low-growing ground covers to shrubby cinquefoils that can reach 4 feet in height.

Showy flowers in shades of purple, blue, red, pink, and white are the hallmark of this vigorous and attractive climber. Some varieties of clematis die back to the ground in winter; others are evergreen or semievergreen.

Coreopsis, or tickseed, is a hardy perennial that produces bright yellow, daisy-like flowers throughout the summer into fall. It is adaptable to most soil types and easy to grow, with a tendency to self-sow. Great as a cut flower.

The daisy-like cosmos comes in a variety of colors. Feathery foliage can grow up to 6 feet tall. An excellent cut flower.

There are many forms of cotoneaster, from low-growing mats to small trees. White, pink, or violet blooms appear in spring, followed by red or black berries.

Common Name	Botanical Name	Type	Zone	Light
crab apple, flowering	*Malus*	deciduous tree	3-8	full sun
crape myrtle	*Lagerstroemia*	deciduous shrub	7-10	full sun
currant, flowering	*Ribes* *Saxifragaceae*	deciduous shrub	2-10	full sun to partial shade
cypress	*Cypressus*	conifer tree	7-8	full sun
daffodil (narcissus)	*Narcissus*	blooming bulb	3-9	full sun to partial shade

Comments

Red, white, or pink blooms appear on the flowering crab apple tree in early spring. Many varieties are quite fragrant, and most produce small fruit that attracts birds.

Crape myrtle produces pink, white, red, or lavender blooms from July to September. It needs a moist, rich, well-drained soil, and grows to heights of 6 to 30 feet.

The flowers of the currant are generally yellow or chartreuse, but some varieties produce red flowers. Spring blooms are followed by edible summer berries.

Associated with Pluto, the god of the underworld in classical mythology, the cypress became a symbol of immortality because it was believed to have the power to preserve bodies. The cypress signified death and mourning in the Victorian language of flowers, and is also associated with death in Chinese lore. It is often planted in cemeteries. The cypress tree tends to have a narrow, upright profile, and can exceed 100 feet in height.

In Greek mythology, Narcissus was a young man who became infatuated with his own reflection in a pool of water. He died from his self-obsession and was transformed into a flower. The ancient Greeks believed that the narcissus, or daffodil, thrived in Hades, hence its long association with death and burial. The Egyptians associated the daffodil with the underworld as well, using the flower in funeral wreaths, and this association reappears in the Victorian language of flowers. Like other spring-blooming bulbs, the daffodil is a symbol of hope and rebirth. The yellow, white, cream, pink, apricot, orange, or red flowers are excellent for cutting.

Common Name	Botanical Name	Type	Zone	Light
dahlia	*Dahlia*	perennial or annual	all	full sun
daphne	*Daphne*	deciduous, semi-evergreen, or evergreen shrub	5-9	full sun to partial shade
daylily	*Hemerocallis*	perennial	3-10	full sun to partial shade
delphinium	*Delphinium*	perennial	3-8	full sun, but not too hot and dry
dianthus (carnation, pink, maiden pink, sweet william)	*Dianthus*	evergreen perennial or annual	3-7	full sun
dill	*Anethum graveolens*	annual herb	all	full sun

Comments

A large family of brightly colored, long-flowering plants, including anemone, ball, cactus, colarette, miniature, mignon, orchid, peony, pompom, single, and water lily types. Tender tubers need to be stored indoors in the winter in most zones.

The daphne symbolized immortality in the Victorian language of flowers. Clusters of small, often fragrant lilac-like flowers appear in spring or early summer, and fruit ripens in the fall. Excellent for rock gardens, borders, or as a specimen plant, but be aware that the fruit, leaves, and bark of the daphne are poisonous.

The daylily comes in a wide variety of colors, including red, maroon, gold, yellow, and orange. Blooming season varies with variety—from early summer to late summer.

The delphinium requires a moist, well-fertilized soil, preferably alkaline. Blooms are various shades of blue, purple, pink, yellow, or white. A wonderful cut flower.

Dianthus is also known as carnation, pink, maiden pink, and sweet william. In Christian legend, the tears that Mary cried at Christ's crucifixion are said to have turned to flowers upon striking the ground; for this reason, maiden pink is sometimes referred to as "the tears of the Virgin Mary." In Italian folklore, the white carnation is associated with death and burial. Flowers are pink, white, red, or bicolor.

Dill is a hardy annual that produces feathery leaves and yellow flower heads on long slender stalks. Highly aromatic, its leaves and seeds are commonly used for pickling.

Common Name	*Botanical Name*	Type	Zone	Light
dogwood, flowering	*Comus*	deciduous tree	5-10	full sun to partial shade
fennel	*Foeniculum vulgare*	annual herb	all	full sun
fig	*Ficus*	deciduous tree (evergreen in warm climates)	7-10	full sun
flax	*Linum*	perennial	3-9	full sun
forget-me-not	*Myosotis*	biennial or annual	3-10	partial shade to shade
forsythia	*Forsythia*	deciduous shrub	4-7	full sun or partial shade
geranium	*Pelargonium*	annual (perennial in zones 9-11)	all	full sun to partial shade

Comments

A popular legend links the flower of the dogwood to the crucifixion of Christ. *Comus florida*, the most common type, produces large white or pink flowers in late spring and red berries in the summer that are relished by birds.

Fennel symbolizes resurrection and rebirth. Although an annual, fennel acts like a perennial in warmer climates.

In India, it is believed that the ghosts of brahmans live in fig trees, which are sacred to the Hindus. In addition to the fig tree, there is a creeping fig, which is an evergreen vine that produces inedible fruit but is excellent for walls and hanging baskets. The weeping fig (*Ficus benjamina*) and the rubber plant (*Ficus elastica*) are both popular evergreen houseplants.

Flax produces blue or yellow flowers from May to September. It will self-sow.

In a European legend, a youth drowns picking this flower for his beloved. His last words are "Forget me not!" A 6- to 12-inch tall spreading plant with tiny, profuse, exquisite blue flowers in the spring.

Clusters of yellow flowers appear on the forsythia in early to mid spring. A vigorous and hardy plant that can be used for hedges or ground cover.

The flower clusters of the geranium are white, pink, or purple. Scented geraniums are typically brought indoors for the winter in all but the warmest climates. Vining types are great for hanging baskets.

Common Name	Botanical Name	Type	Zone	Light
germander	*Teucrium chamaedrys*	deciduous shrub	5-10	full sun
gladiolus	*Gladiolus*	flowering bulb/ annual	all	full sun
globe amaranth	*Gomphrena*	annual	all	full sun to partial shade
grape	*Vitis*	perennial vine	3-10	full sun
hawthorn	*Crataegus*	deciduous tree	3-6	full sun to partial shade
holly	*Ilex*	evergreen shrub	6-9	full sun to partial shade
hollyhock	*Alcea rosea*	annual; biennial in milder zones	2-9	full sun

Comments

Once established, the hardy germander requires little water and will tolerate poor soil. Purple, pink, or white flowers appear in late spring and summer.

The gladiolus blooms 60 to 100 days after planting. Its flowers are white, purple, red, yellow, or orange. An excellent cut flower.

The globe amaranth symbolized immortality and unfading love in the Victorian language of flowers. White, pink, purple, orange, or red flowers appear throughout the summer.

Grapevines can be grown on an arbor, fence, or trellis. There are many types and hybrids, all of which require about 5 months of frost-free weather to ripen fruit.

In Celtic folklore, the hawthorn, named for its sharp thorns, is associated with everlasting life. It produces white flowers in the spring and red or scarlet fruit in the fall. In the fall, its leaves turn red and gold.

Holly is a traditional symbol for renewal, resurrection, and eternal life. It produces small white flowers in spring, followed, in most varieties, by bright red berries in the fall. Leaves are glossy green. Though it grows slowly, it can exceed 30 feet at maturity.

The hollyhock produces white, apricot, yellow, purple, red, pink, or maroon flowers in summer. It self-sows so easily, it is considered a perennial in some zones.

Common Name	Botanical Name	Type	Zone	Light
honeysuckle	*Lonicera*	perennial vine or deciduous shrub	3-10	full sun to partial shade
hyacinth	*Hyacinthus orientalis*	blooming bulb	all	full sun to partial shade
hydrangea	*Hydrangea*	deciduous shrub	3-8	full sun to partial shade
iris	*Iridaceae*	perennial	3-10	full sun
ivy	*Hedera*	evergreen perennial vine	5-10	full sun to shade

Comments

Honeysuckle is prized for its fragrant flowers, whether used as a climbing vine, ground cover, or specimen plant. Birds are attracted to its fleshy berries. Some types of honeysuckle are evergreen or semievergreen.

In Greek mythology, Hyacinthus was a young Spartan prince whom a jealous god killed. From his blood Apollo caused a flower to grow that supposedly displayed the Greek word for "woe" on its petals and leaves. In the Victorian language of flowers, the purple hyacinth signified sorrow. Very fragrant blooms of purple, blue, pink, cream, salmon, white, or red flowers appear in the spring.

The hydrangea produces large clusters of small flowers—white, purple, blue, or pink—in early to late summer, depending on the variety. It dies back during the winter in colder zones.

In Greek mythology, the goddess Iris accompanied the dead to the afterlife. The flower came to represent a link between the living and the dead and was often placed on graves. The white iris, indicating the purity of the soul, is traditionally planted on the graves of Muslims. Depending on the variety, blooms will appear from spring to early summer. The iris comes in an extraordinary range of colors.

Like many evergreens, ivy is a symbol of rebirth, immortality, and everlasting love. Ivy is also traditionally associated with healing. An effective ground cover that will hold soil on slopes, preventing erosion.

Common Name	Botanical Name	Type	Zone	Light
lamb's ear	Stachys lanata	perennial	4	full sun to partial shade
larkspur	Consolida	annual	all	full sun, with some shade in hot areas
laurel (bay)	Laurus	evergreen shrub or perennial herb	7-10	full sun to partial shade
lavender	Lavandula	perennial	4-9	full sun
lilac	Syringa	deciduous shrub	2-8	full sun to partial shade
lily	Lilium	blooming bulb	all	full sun to partial shade

Comments

Lamb's ear—a type of stachys or betony—is a low-growing, spreading plant that produces small purplish or reddish flowers in summer. Its leaves are soft, silvery, and felt-like, hence the name. A lovely complement to pastel-colored gardens.

The larkspur can bloom throughout the growing season if sown at three-week intervals. Its flowers are blue, purple, lavender, pink, red, or white.

The ancient Greeks often used laurel, or bay, in funeral wreaths, and laurel has long been connected with death and the afterlife. An easily shaped, vigorous plant with fragrant dark leaves. Tiny white flowers appear in early summer, followed by small black berries in the fall.

The fragrant aroma of lavender has been thought to provide comfort for the grieving soul, and the plant is symbolically associated with memories and peace. The blooms are lavender, blue, violet, or purple. An excellent flower for drying.

The lilac produces remarkably fragrant clusters of small flowers in shades of purple, lavender, pink, or white, blooming in late spring to early summer. Many varieties are available. Lilac grows well in almost any soil and is often used for hedges.

The lily is a traditional symbol for death and the transition of the soul to the afterlife, so it is often used in funerals and memorials. Tombs in the ancient city of Pompei featured lilies as remembrances for the dead. In one Spanish legend, a lily grows from

Common Name	*Botanical Name*	Type	Zone	Light
lily-of-the-valley	*Convallaria majalis*	perennial	2-8	shade to partial shade
locust	*Robinia*	deciduous tree	all	full sun
lupine	*Lupinus*	perennial	4-8	full sun to partial shade
marigold	*Tagetes*	annual	all	full sun

Comments

the heart of a devout young Christian after he is buried. Folklore has it that the soul becomes a lily upon death. Another legend tells how a lily was moved to tears for Christ in the Garden of Gethsemane; a tear remains in each bloom today, a symbol of grief and humility. Hardy lilies come in many colors; all die back after flowering.

The lily-of-the-valley is a symbol of resurrection, often specifically linked with Christ's resurrection. Extremely fragrant white or pink bell-shaped flowers appear in spring. An excellent ground cover for shady areas near buildings, fences, or trees.

The locust tree symbolized "affection beyond the grave" in the Victorian language of flowers. White or pink flowers appear in spring, followed by red or blue berries.

The lupine grows up to 5 feet tall, with long spikes of flowers in a wide array of colors: white, cream, yellow, pink, blue, red, orange, purple, and bicolor. The blooms appear in late spring to early summer.

In some folk cultures of both Asia and Europe, the marigold has been thought to soothe a sorrowful heart. For the Victorians, the marigold symbolized grief and remembrance. Many varieties are available, from dwarf varieties to plants that can grow up to 4 feet tall. The marigold is very hardy and easy to grow. It blooms continuously throughout the growing season in shades from pale yellow to deep gold and maroon. Scented types are often used to repel garden pests.

Common Name	*Botanical Name*	Type	Zone	Light
marjoram	*Origanum*	annual herb in northern zones; perennial in warmer climates	all	full sun
mint	*Mentha*	perennial herb	all	full sun to partial shade
morning-glory	*Ipomoea purpurea*	annual vine	all	full sun
moss, Irish	*Arenaria verna* or *Sagina subulata*	perennial	2-10	full sun to partial shade
myrtle	*Myrtus*	evergreen shrub	9-10	full sun to partial shade
nasturtium	*Tropaeolum*	annual	all	full sun to partial shade

Comments

Marjoram was planted by the ancient Greeks on graves to help the dead sleep peacefully. Sweet marjoram (*Origanum majorana*) is the most common garden species; pot marjoram (*Origanum onites*) is hardier but smaller. Grown both for its fragrance and use in cooking, marjoram can be used for border plantings.

Use caution when planting a mint; it can become very invasive. Plant where it will have boundaries, or use a pot sunk into the ground.

The twining vines of the morning-glory have large, heart-shaped leaves and blue, red, pink, white, purple, or bicolored flowers that bloom every morning once the plant is established. Be aware that the seeds of the morning-glory can become invasive.

"Irish moss" is the common name for two similar species: *Arenaria verna*, also known as moss sandwort, and *Sagina subulata*, also known as Corsican pearlwort. Both produce small white flowers in summer and are often used as ground cover.

The myrtle is traditionally associated with immortality. The leaves of the myrtle are fragrant when crushed. White or pink flowers appear in spring or summer; dark berries appear in the fall.

The nasturtium grows 12 to 18 inches tall, with some climbing varieties growing even taller. Its flowers come in shades of cream, yellow, orange, red, gold, and maroon.

Common Name	Botanical Name	Type	Zone	Light
nemophila (baby-blue-eyes)	Nemophila	annual	all	full sun to partial shade
oak	Quercus	deciduous tree	3-10	full sun
oregano	Origanum vulgare	perennial herb	3-10	full sun
palm	numerous genera	evergreen tree	10	full sun
pansy	Viola tricolor	annual or biennial	all	full sun to partial shade
parsley	Petroselinum crispum	annual or biennial herb	all	full sun to partial shade
passionflower	Passiflora caerulea	evergreen or semi-evergreen vine	5-10	full sun

Comments

The light-blue blooms of nemophila, or baby-blue-eyes, appear from mid-spring through early summer. The plant grows in mounds 6 to 12 inches wide and tall.

The Druids believed that the dead resided inside of oak trees. In Western culture, the acorn has traditionally been associated with immortality. A majestic, long-lived tree.

Oregano produces small lovely purple or pink flowers in summer. A beautiful but hardy plant that's easy to grow and has many culinary uses.

A palm branch was the symbol of the ancient Egyptian god of eternity, Heh. A traditional symbol of victory, the palm branch represents Christ's victory over death in Christian mythology. It is also a symbol of the Christian garden of paradise. Most types will not tolerate freezing temperatures. Often grown as a houseplant.

The name "pansy" comes from the French *pensee* for thoughts or remembrance. From the same genera (*Viola*) as the violet, the pansy is ideal for borders, rock gardens, and spring-flowering bulb gardens.

For the ancient Greeks, parsley was a symbol of death that was often used in funeral wreaths. It is a compact plant, good for edging.

The passionflower is a vigorous vine that can grow up to 20 feet in length. Large white flowers tinged with pink or lavender appear in summer. Popular in the South, some cold-resistant varieties are available as well.

Common Name	*Botanical Name*	Type	Zone	Light
pearly everlasting	*Anaphalis margaritacea*	perennial	3-8	full sun
peony	*Paeonia*	perennial	2-8	full sun to partial shade
peppermint	*Mentha piperita*	perennial herb	all	full sun to partial shade
periwinkle	*Vinca minor*	evergreen perennial	4-9	partial shade to full shade
persimmon	*Diospyros*	deciduous tree	6-10	full sun
petunia	*Petunia*	annual or tender perennial	all	full sun

Comments

The pearly everlasting prefers a moist, rich soil. It blooms in late summer. Its button-like flowers are pearly white; its foliage is gray-green. A good cut flower. Also, a good dried flower for winter arrangements.

The peony has traditionally been considered a healing plant. Its large, exceptionally fragrant flowers can be white or one of many shades of red. The peony blooms from mid-spring into early summer and requires little care.

Peppermint has invasive qualities. Use caution where you plant it, or plant it in a pot and sink the pot into the ground

Periwinkle produces lavender-blue flowers in summer on trailing vines. A spreading ground cover, good for slopes or shady areas, but potentially quite invasive.

In the Victorian language of flowers, the persimmon signified "Bury me amid nature's beauties." Although *Diospyros virginiana* is native to the Southeastern United States, the persimmon tree is rarely cultivated here. Also called "possumwood" because possums like to feast on persimmon fruit.

Petunia is a popular annual for many reasons: its many shapes, sizes, and colors; its fragrance; its long-blooming period; and its versatility in gardens, borders, and hanging baskets.

Common Name	Botanical Name	Type	Zone	Light
phlox	*Phlox*	perennial	2-10	full sun to partial shade
pincushion flower (scabiosa)	*Scabiosa*	perennial or annual	all	full sun
pine	*Pinus*	coniferous tree or shrub	3-10	full sun
plum	*Prunus mume*	deciduous tree	3-10	full sun
poinsettia	*Euphorbia*	annual	all	full sun to partial shade
poppy	*Papaver*	perennial or annual	all	full sun

Comments

Phlox produces flowers in shades of magenta, white, lavender, pink, or red. Creeping phlox is a hardy, low-growing plant with needle-like foliage—an excellent ground cover for slopes. Larger varieties grow up to 4 feet tall. All are easy to cultivate.

The pincushion flower, or scabiosa, gets its common name from its pincushion-like blue, crimson, pink, lavender, or white blooms. Can be grown as a perennial in most parts of the country. A fragrant, long-lasting cut flower.

In China, the pine tree symbolizes the triumph of virtue over adversity and the eternal cycle of life and death. In Western cultures, it is associated, along with evergreens generally, with everlasting life. Some pine trees can grow over 100 feet tall. Smaller pines, like the dwarf mugo, are good for foundation plantings or as specimen plants.

In China, the plum symbolizes hope and rebirth. There are many varieties, with varying degrees of hardiness. The dwarf varieties are better suited for most gardens.

A common houseplant at Christmas time, this compact shrub can be planted outdoors as an annual. Ornamental leaves and bracts turn from bright green to red, pink, or white under appropriate conditions.

Garlands of poppies were placed on mummies in ancient Egypt. Ancient Greeks also crowned their dead with poppies. In Europe, legend has it that poppies spring up on battlefields from the blood of slain soldiers, hence their association with veterans of wars. The poppy symbolized consolation, sleep, and rest in the Victorian language of

Common Name	Botanical Name	Type	Zone	Light
primrose	*Primula*	perennial	3-5	partial shade; won't tolerate extreme heat or cold
purple coneflower	*Echinacea*	perennial wildflower	3-9	full sun to partial shade
pussytoes	*Antennaria*	perennial	4-10	full sun
pussy willow	*Salix*	deciduous shrub or tree	2-10	full sun

Comments

flowers and was commonly used to memorialize the dead. The oriental poppy (*Papaver orientale*) produces striking flowers in a rainbow of colors in early summer. The alpine poppy (*Papaver alpinum*) is good for rock gardens and retaining walls.

In Greek mythology, primrose was called "paralisos" for the son of Flora and Priapus, who died mourning the death of his betrothed. The primrose was given to the earth by Flora and Priapus as a living memorial to their son. Because it symbolized sadness in the Victorian language of flowers, primrose was often planted on the graves of children. Colors include pink, red, scarlet, purple, white, yellow, and lavender.

The hardy purple coneflower produces large purple flowers on stalks up to 4 feet tall from summer into fall. The flowers attract butterflies; birds are drawn to the seed heads after the petals fall off.

Pussytoes grows in a low spreading mat. Delicate gray and pink flowers appear in summer. Pussytoes is named for its soft woolly gray leaves, which resemble cat feet.

The quick-growing pussy willow produces its distinctive catkins in early spring. Depending on the type, the new catkins may appear silver, gray, white, or rose; but all eventually turn yellow with pollen. The common pussy willow (*S. discolor*) can grow over 20 feet tall. Dried catkins are often used in floral displays.

Common Name	Botanical Name	Type	Zone	Light
rhododendron (azalea)	*Rhododendron*	deciduous or evergreen shrub	3-8	full sun to partial shade
rose	*Rosa*	perennial shrub	3-10	full sun to partial shade
rosemary	*Rosmarinus officinalis*	perennial herb	6-11	full sun
rudbeckia (coneflower)	*Rudbeckia*	perennial	3-9	full sun to partial shade
rue (herb of grace)	*Ruta*	perennial herb	4-10	full sun to partial shade
Russian sage	*Perovskia*	perennial	3-10	full sun

Comments

Rhododendron is a large family that includes the azaleas. Rhododendrons are prized for their profuse blooms of rose, crimson, white, orange, scarlet, red, yellow, pink, salmon, violet, bicolor, and mixed color flowers.

The belief that only a single red rose can pass with a human soul from this world to the next is quite ancient. The Egyptians decorated their tombs with roses, and in more modern times, roses have traditionally been placed or dropped on graves. In Christian legend, a rose with eight petals represented resurrection or rebirth. Roses come in many colors, sizes, and types, including hybrid tea roses, floribundas, grandifloras, miniatures, and climbing roses. An incomparable cut flower.

Rosemary is a traditional symbol of remembrance, as Ophelia remarks in Shakespeare's *Hamlet*. The herb has highly aromatic leaves and small lavender-blue or white flowers that appear in early spring.

The daisy-like rudbeckia, or coneflower, grows 2 to 3 feet tall, with yellow or orange flowers that have cone-shaped cores. A good cut flower.

Rue, also known as herb of grace, is a shrub-like perennial with aromatic blue-green leaves and small yellow-green flowers. It is sometimes used to repel insects.

The drought-resistant Russian sage will die back to the ground in northern zones, but will grow back from roots. Long spikes of luminous blue-violet flowers appear in summer.

Common Name	Botanical Name	Type	Zone	Light
sage	*Salvia officinalis*	perennial or annual herb	all	full sun
salvia (scarlet sage, meadow sage)	*Salvia*	perennial or annual	all	full sun
shasta daisy	*Chrysanthemum maximum*	perennial	4-10	full sun to partial shade
silver-lace vine	*Polygonum*	deciduous vine	4-10	full sun
snowdrop	*Galanthus*	blooming bulb	all	full sun to partial shade
spruce	*Picea*	evergreen tree	2-8	full sun to partial shade
sunflower	*Helianthus*	annual	all	full sun

Comments

Sage was considered to have healing properties in ancient Greek culture. It has been used for centuries for both medicinal and culinary purposes.

Often grown as an annual, salvia also has several perennial varieties that are hardy to Zone 4. The flowering spikes of the salvia come in brilliant shades of red, purple, blue, and white.

The shasta daisy is a vigorous plant that produces an abundance of beautiful white blooms throughout the summer. An excellent cut flower.

The small flowers that form on this vigorous twining vine are attractive to bees.

The snowdrop is a traditional emblem of death in Christian mythology. During the Renaissance, the hanging head of the flower was used to represent the Virgin Mary's sorrow over Christ's crucifixion. The three inner petals of the flower are said to look like a death shroud. In the Victorian language of flowers, the snowdrop symbolizes hope. White bell-shaped flowers appear in early spring.

Be mindful of the eventual size of the spruce when placing it in your landscape. Some varieties grow only 5 to 6 feet tall; others grow as tall as 150 feet.

The sunflower is a symbol of remembrance and rebirth. Some varieties reach 10 feet, with flower heads that can exceed a foot in width. The colors of the flowers include yellow, orange, gold, and bicolor. Leave seed heads on to attract birds.

Common Name	*Botanical Name*	Type	Zone	Light
sycamore	*Platanus*	deciduous tree	5-10	full sun
sweet pea	*Lathyrus odoratus*	annual	all	full sun to partial shade
tansy	*Tanacetum*	perennial herb	3-10	full sun
thrift	*Armeria maritima*	perennial	3-9	full sun; some shade in warmer climates
thyme	*Thymus*	perennial	3-10	full sun
trumpet vine	*Campsis*	perennial vine	4-10	full sun
tulip	*Tulipa*	blooming bulb	4-8	full sun to partial shade
viburnum	*Viburnum*	deciduous and evergreen shrub	2-10	full sun to partial shade

Comments

In ancient Egypt, sycamores were believed to form the eastern gate of heaven and were often planted near tombs or used as wood for coffins. These large trees provide excellent shade.

There are many varieties of this popular annual, which can be used as a climbing vine or border plant, or in beds and window boxes. A good cut flower.

Tansy can be used as an herb or dried flower.

The thrift symbolized sympathy in the Victorian language of flowers. Rose-pink or white flowers appear in late spring and last into summer. Good for rock gardens and edgings. Also known as sea pink.

Thyme can be grown as an herb, border plant, or ground cover. Its aromatic evergreen leaves and small purple flowers make it as ornamental as it is useful.

Th large trumpet-like blooms of this fast-growing vine attract hummingbirds.

In Islam, the tulip is a traditional symbol for the death of a martyr. Tulips come in many colors: red, yellow, white, pink, lavender, purple, and cream. A wonderful cut flower.

The viburnum, or cranberry bush, produces long-lasting pink or white fragrant blooms in late spring to early summer, followed by red or black berries in the fall. The fruit is very attractive to birds.

Common Name	Botanical Name	Type	Zone	Light
violet	*Viola*	perennial/ annual	3-5	partial shade
Virgina creeper (woodbine, American ivy)	*Parthenocissus or Ampelopsis*	perennial vine or ground cover	3-10	full sun to partial shade
walnut	*Julgans*	deciduous tree	5-8	full sun
water lily	*Nymphaea*	perennial	3-10	full sun
willow, weeping	*Salix babylonica*	deciduous tree	5-8	full sun

Comments

In Greek mythology, Ajax committed suicide when he failed to avenge his friend Hector's death. Where his blood dropped on the ground, violets appeared—a living tribute to their friendship. The Romans used violets to decorate tombs. In Christian legend, violets were white until the crucifixion of Christ, when, to reflect Mary's grief, they turned purple—a color traditionally associated with mourning. Blue, purple, rose, or white flowers complement the deep green foliage of the heart-shaped leaves on this charming low-grower. The fragrant flowers bloom in early spring.

This quick-growing creeping vine produces bluish-black berries that birds adore. The leaves turn bright red in the fall before dropping off.

The walnut tree is traditionally associated with funerals. The slow-growing black walnut (*Juglans nigra*) does not make a good lawn tree because its roots emit toxins that can damage surrounding plants. Plant in pairs for better nut production.

Hardy water lilies can survive outdoors as long as the roots are protected by water or soil from freezing. Tropical lilies require frost-free weather.

As is the case with many "weeping" plants, the weeping willow is a traditional symbol for mourning. In Celtic folklore, the willow was associated with death. This graceful pendulous tree grows well in wet areas.

Common Name	*Botanical Name*	Type	Zone	Light
yarrow	*Achillea*	perennial	3-8	full sun
yew	*Taxus*	evergreen shrub	3-7	full sun to partial shade
zinnia	*Zinnia*	annual	all	full sun

Comments

The yarrow is traditionally associated with healing. Its fern-like foliage forms an attractive background for clusters of bright white, yellow, pink, or red flowers that bloom from summer through fall. In addition to attracting butterflies, it makes a great cut or dried flower.

In Celtic folklore, the yew symbolized death, rebirth, and immortality. It was placed on graves as a reminder that death is but a transition to a new life. In the Victorian language of flowers, the yew symbolized sorrow. The needles of the yew are about an inch long, dark green, and lustrous. Red berries ripen in the fall. A fine foundation plant that can be easily shaped.

The zinnia produces dahlia- and daisy-like blossoms in many colors and sizes. Reliable, easy to grow, and long blooming. A nice cut flower.